TRADE-UPS

HOW TO GAIN TRACTION IN A WORLD OF ENDLESS DIGITAL DISTRACTION

CLAY CLARK
WITH JONATHAN KELLY

Learn how to optimize your happiness while also freeing up at least 11 hours per day (77 hours per week, 4,004 hours per year, and 18.28 years of your life).

. . . .

Learn how to decrease the amount of hours you spend interacting with the people you like the least.

. . . .

Learn how to gain traction in a world of relentless digital distractions.

. . . .

Learn how to free yourself from the digital leash (your smartphone) that is directly related to dramatically increasing the distractions, depression and dissonance that you are experiencing on a daily basis.

. . . .

Learn why smartphones are making people depressed, distracted, and dumb and how to free yourself from the destruction and dystopia that these devices create.

. . . .

LEARN HOW SUPER SUCCESSFUL PEOPLE GAIN TRACTION IN A WORLD OF ENDLESS DISTRACTION.

Throughout my career, my partner and I have been blessed and fortunate enough to build 15 multi-million dollar businesses and we've been able to do it because we don't waste our time doing activities that don't get us closer to our goals. We don't waste time passionately going in the wrong direction. We don't waste time implementing systems that don't work and we don't waste 11 hours per day engaged in digital debates, digital distraction, and the digital dystopia that consumes the days of most people.

What Would You Do with an Additional 11 Hours Per Day

If you were able to gain 11 hours of your life back per day, do you think that you would be able to get more things done? Think about this for a second. What if I was actually able to teach YOU how to get 11 hours per day of your life back. Would that change things? Having coached people and businesses to success since the age of 27 after selling my first business www.DJConnection.com I can passionately, personally and accurately tell you that the number one reason or excuse that most people provide for failing to be able to get things done that need to be done is that they ran out of time, didn't have the time or couldn't find the time.

NOTABLE QUOTABLE

"The quality of your life is directly affected by how and where you spend your time."

LEE COCKERELL

(The former Executive Vice President of Walt Disney World resorts who once was directly responsible for managing 40,000 employees and 1,000,000 guests per week)

During the pages of this book I am going to teach you how to make the TRADE-UPS needed to become more focused so that you can minimize the distractions that are standing in the way of the action steps that you need to take to achieve your goals!

FUN FACT:

Did you know that according to Nielsen, the average American adult now spends 11 hours per day interacting with media?

https://www.nielsen.com/us/en/insights/article/2018/time-flies-us-adults-now-spend-nearly-half-a-day-interacting-with-media

Trade-Ups | How to Gain Traction in a World of Endless Distraction

TRADE UPS

HOW TO GAIN TRACTION IN A WORLD OF ENDLESS DIGITAL DISTRACTIONS

Caution: To read this life-changing book you will have to put your smartphone down don't worry, you won't die).

CLAY CLARK
WITH JONATHAN KELLY

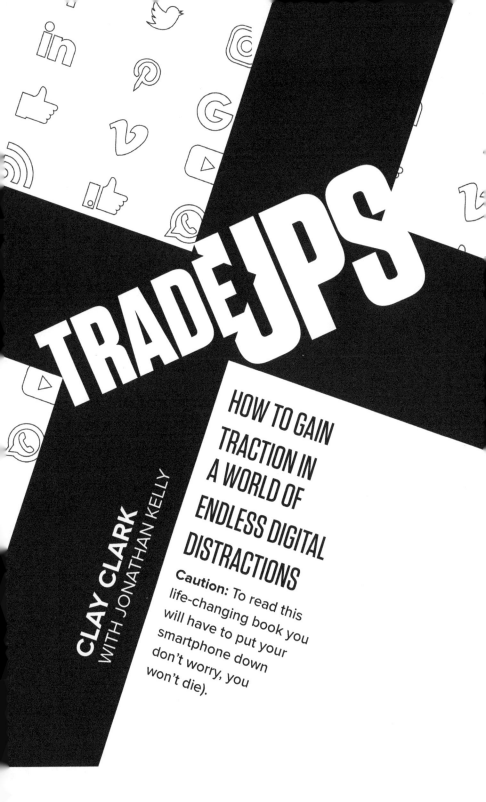

For Clay, who has forever changed my view
of what it means to live a full and happy life.

TABLE OF CONTENTS

Introduction - What are Trade-Ups? (Wasted Time is a Wasted Life)

. . . .

Chapter 1 - Determine Your F6 Goals Today or You Are F'd

. . . .

Chapter 2 - Design Your Days (The Art of Morning Meta Mapping)

. . . .

Chapter 3 - What Gets Scheduled Gets Done

. . . .

Chapter 4 - You Must Say No to Grow (Defining Your Digital Boundaries)

. . . .

Chapter 5 - Being Present Is a Present (Don't Text
While Driving, Working or Having Sex)

. . . .

Chapter 6 - Don't Allow the Almond-Sized Part of
Your Brain to Control Your Whole Life

. . . .

Chapter 7 - Don't Let the Trolls Be in Control

. . . .

Chapter 8 - Smartphone Fasting - The Power of Weekly Digital Detoxing

. . . .

Chapter 9 - F.O.C.U.S. on Traction Producing Activities

. . . .

Chapter 10 - Start Now, Some Day Is Not in Your Calendar

. . . .

INTRODUCTION:

What are Trade-Ups?
(Wasted Time is a Wasted Life)

In our world of perpetual distraction, how do the most successful people find the time to get it all done? If you are not intentional, the world that you let in will control your life. There are countless notifications, emails, social media updates and endless distractions that are going to consume the vast majority of your days if you allow them to. In this book I aim to teach you the Trade-Ups you can take in order to gain the traction required to get stuff done and to find the time needed to achieve your goals.

> This means that you say "no" to the things that steal time so you can say "yes" to the things that maximize your time.

On the planet Earth it would appear that we all have just 24 hours per day and 7 days per week to turn our dreams into reality. Based upon my 39 years of research on the planet Earth, it appears as though Oprah, Steve Jobs, Steve Harvey, YOU and I have the same 24 hours per day to get things done. So, how are successful people able to find the time needed to get things done while unsuccessful people can't seem to ever find enough time? The answer is Trade-Ups! The average person that you will meet on the street spent all day yesterday responding to the "birthday" updates and messages they received on Facebook, emails from random people, looking at the endless push notifications sent from social media, engaging with the countless incoming calls and texts, and essentially wasting valuable time. In order to achieve success, YOU must make Trade-Ups. This means that you say "no" to the things that steal time so you can say "yes" to the things that maximize your time. Essentially you must learn to learn to say "no" to grow! This requires focus and intentionality as you begin to identify the action steps that are your highest and best use, in order for you to achieve your goals.

I promise that you will survive if you don't look at your device.

We can easily see examples of this all throughout our world. NBA players are not checking their phones during games. When Lebron James is showcasing his basketball skills and leading his team on an NBA Christmas day "special" he is simultaneously making necessary trade-ups. While he is putting on this "Christmas Basketball Laser Show" for us all to see, he is NOT also simultaneously opening up gifts with his kids under the tree. He is trading-up one choice for another. When a skilled cardiovascular surgeon is performing a life-saving open heart surgery on someone's mother, he cannot also be focused on also attending his kids soccer game. The surgeon has to also make the trade-ups needed to save someone's life.

The President of the United States is unreachable while he is delivering a State of the Union Address, even by his own family. Earlier today, before I was writing this book, I made a glorious trade-up and chose to have sex with my wife rather than to write the words found within this book.

Are you saying that I didn't write the words found within this book while also simultaneously having marital sex? Yes. True. I did not write any portion of this book while simultaneously having sex with my wife. I am confident you are grateful for this fact. In order for you to achieve massive success, you TOO must learn how to control your time so that you can focus on the things that matter the most as you travel on this path to your goals.

The F6 Life

I think that we are all in agreement that everybody has just 24 hours in each day and it's how we trade-up those 24 hours that is the CRITICAL determinant of whether we have success in any given area of our life. Thus, learning how to effectively manage your time is the GAME-CHANGING SKILL that we need to master.

So, let's first begin with the end in mind. I want you to take a moment to think about your goals for your faith, family, finances, fitness, friendship and fun. As you are doing this, just know that by default, in any area where you don't have goals, you will drift, because no one drifts towards super success. Success requires intentionality and success is the enemy of entropy and drifting.

What Gets Scheduled Gets Done.

Reality check; I know that you are busy and that right now you feel tempted to check your email, your social media push notifications and every app notification possible that is being pushed to your phone, but for just a moment, I want you to resist the urge to look at your phone and dream out loud. Actually think about where you want your life to be in the areas of your faith, family, finances, fitness, friendship and fun in the next 12 months. I promise that you will survive if you don't look at your device. We will talk more about this later, and dive into writing down the specifics. At this moment, just allow yourself to dream about the possibilities.

Design Your Days (The Art of Morning Meta Mapping)

Now that you know where you want to be in 12 months in the F6 areas of your life, we must take the time to actually schedule these aspects of your life into your calendar. However, you can't be in two places at one time, unless you are a deity. Therefore, you are going to have to learn to become skilled at what you allow into your schedule. By default, any open space in your schedule will fill up with something. The "somethings" that fill these spots usually consist of time wasting activities. You have the ability to change this in your life today.

What Gets Scheduled Gets Done. Let's get started dealing with Mondays. To be fair, I will share with you a screenshot of my Monday calendar so that you will have a practical example that is real and not theoretical.

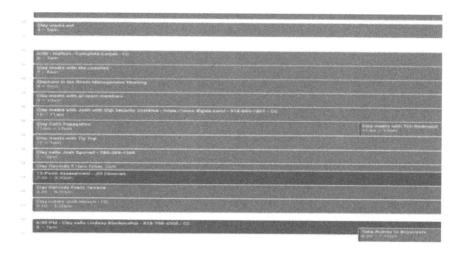

What you see above is my actual Monday calendar. Yes, I do sincerely wake up at 3 AM every day (at this point in my life). Yes, my first client really does experience my one-on-one coaching at 6 AM. Yes, his real company is actually called Complete Carpet. When I am meeting with Nathan, I am not sleeping in or doing something else. When I meet with Nathan, I am able to be mentally and physically present the entire time, because I have chosen to schedule that meeting in my calendar so that I can give him the attention needed to grow his business.

When you allow the distractions in the world to control your schedule and are constantly having your focus pulled in a million different directions, the quality of what you are doing decreases.

I choose to be emotionally, intellectually, spiritually and financially invested in Nathans success from 6 AM - 7 AM. Because of this, at 7 AM, I am able to switch gears. At 7 AM, I coach my employees and my teammates to be the best business plan implementers that they can possibly be. If I allowed my schedule to control me, then I would not be able to do this. You too must intentionally design your day. Designing your day will require you to trade-up less valuable uses of your time for the most important uses. Doing this requires a morning META time where you go over your calendar and plan the needed action items that you will accomplish that day. Meta time involves going over the "rocks" and the "sand" in your schedule.

Meta time involves going over the "rocks" and the "sand" in your schedule.

Rocks are the immovable blocks of time that you have committed to something intentional, like a meeting with a client. Sand is the list of "to-do" items that must get done, but can be accomplished in the spaces between the rocks. However, none of this will be possible until you first take the time to create a schedule and a to-do list.

A powerful key to my success and to the success of the millionaires and billionaires that I have interviewed on the Thrivetime Show Podcast is that "success people" intentionally plan out each hour, day and moment of their lives. Super successful people do not go to work to "just see what is going to happen."

If you look at my calendar at 2:00 PM today, I am going to interview the *New York Times* best-selling author T. Harv Ecker. Then at 2:30 PM I am going to be meeting with the legendary founder of the celebrity loved brand, Rustic Cuff (Jill Donovan) about the action steps that she needs to take to get her online marketing presence to the next level. You might be wondering, "Well Clay, who makes that schedule?" I do. You may be wondering, "What if someone calls you?"

My phone is not near me for nearly 90% of my day. Why? Because I am focused and focus to me stands for: Focusing On Key Actions Until Success. In fact, just for fun, as I was writing this, I went ahead and turned my smartphone back on just for a second to see how many potential interruptions I've traded-up today in order to **CREATE THE TIME NEEDED** to write this book. Here is what I missed:

> **FUN FACT:**
> While writing / editing this book on October 12th of 2019 I have personally missed 11 calls, 40 emails, 34 Facebook updates, 27 text messages and haven't even looked at Twitter, Linkedin, Youtube, or Instagram.

Because I know that Inc. Magazine was correct when they wrote, "It Takes 23 Minutes to Recover From a Distraction at Work", I simply do not allow time for random humans or people to reach me throughout my day. At this specific moment, as I am writing this book, I refuse to allow work related calls and business clients to reach me. When I am at home, I have scheduled my time to be there.

It would not be right of me to allow others to steal this time from being invested into my highest and best use. Do I have a super-power when it comes to blocking out time? No. I literally just turn my phone onto airplane mode.

Truth be told, my phone is in airplane mode 90% of the time.

Why? Because I want to be intentional about with whom and where I am investing my time. You and I only live once and I have no interest in spending my life responding to digital distractions and push notifications. I choose to trade-up those things for a better life.

FUN FACT

Time Flies: U.S. Adults Now Spend Nearly Half a Day Interacting with Media.
https://www.nielsen.com/us/en/insights/
article/2018/time-flies-us-adults-now-spend-
nearly-half-a-day-interacting-with-media/

When you take the time to schedule the rocks and sand that needs to get done, you are giving yourself the foundation needed to be able to say "no" to the unnecessary distractions. What do you use to manage your schedule? I use Google calendar. It is free and easy to use. Find a way to manage your schedule asap!

You Must Say No to Grow (Defining Your Digital Boundaries)

I realize that in America, much of today's education system involves memorization and regurgitation. Read this, remember that, now take this test and repeat. However, life outside of academia and specifically life as an entrepreneur involves problem solving and implementation. Thus, because I am an entrepreneur at my core, my entire focus is on helping you to implement the proven time freedom creating systems, strategies and processes that actually work.

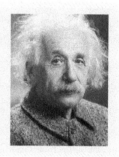

NOTABLE QUOTABLE

"Education is what remains after one has forgotten what one has learned in school."

ALBERT EINSTEIN

(The german-born theoretical physicist who developed the theory of relativity, one of the two pillars of modern physics (alongside quantum mechanics.)

Living a happy life requires trade-ups and even writing this book requires trade-ups. As I am physically typing out the pages of this book, my son is mowing a path in our 15+ acre backyard / forest to create a walking path for his friends to enjoy when we have his back-to-school celebration. In order for us to enjoy cooking "S'Mores" with his friends, he too had to make the trade-ups needed to say "no" to social media, time with the grandmas and to do anything other than to create the path needed for his friends to safely and easily make the walk from the back of our home to the incredible fire pit.

So, the real question is...when will YOU create the time needed to write your book, to mow your path through the fields and live a life that you have INTENTIONALLY DESIGNED? Basically what I am asking is when will YOU choose to say "no?"

Being Present Is a Present (Don't Text While Driving, Working or Having Sex)

Constant Connection is a Recipe for No Progression, NoConnection and Depression. Throughout the pages of this book, my goal is to teach you the Trade-Ups Principle that I taught my clients to help them grow their businesses on average by 30% annually, while also helping them to **DRAMATICALLY** increase the level of both financial and time freedom that they have in their lives. Since selling my first business, DJConnection.com, at the age of 27, I have served as a business coach to help my clients implement the proven systems, processes and strategies that work time and time again.

...Smartphones are robbing my clients and nearly every human on the planet of their time freedom...

Yet, over the past 5 years I've noticed a disturbing trend that is getting worse and worse all of the time. By default, smartphones are robbing my clients and nearly every human on the planet of their time freedom, regardless of how much money they make.

I have noticed that smartphones are killing people, dreams, time and so much more. Maybe it is time to trade-up that smartphone for something better.

NOTABLE QUOTABLE

"We need to re-create boundaries. When you carry a digital gadget that creates a virtual link to the office, you need to create a virtual boundary that didn't exist before."

DANIEL GOLEMAN

(The *New York Times* best-selling author of Emotional Intelligence and a recipient of the Career Achievement award for Excellence in the Media (1984) from the American Psychological Association)

Don't Allow the Almond-Sized Part of Your Brain to Control Your Whole Life

When starting my first business out of my parents' basement at the age of 16, I was confronted with the harsh reality that we all have just 24 hours in a day. As I grew the little business, I struggled to keep up with my school work, to play basketball at a competitive level and to start a profitable entertainment empire. I found myself constantly running out of time. I had to make a painful, yet profitable and life-changing TRADE-UP.

I decided to quit playing basketball, to quit hanging out with people that were busy going nowhere (but to parties and clubs) and to become intentional about where I was spending each and every hour of each and every day.

The amygdala in an almond shaped part of the brain that processes our emotions. This is the part of the brain that is put in charge of how you cope with the world around you.

Be encouraged to know that as you trade-up distractions, like your smartphone, your overall mental health will improve.

When you allow too many distractions into your life and you do not set healthy boundaries, the amygdala becomes overloaded and it becomes nearly impossible to process data in a logical way. When you make the necessary trade-ups in your life, you are setting boundaries for your amygdala and giving yourself the ability to make better decisions. Be encouraged to know that as you trade-up distractions, like your smartphone, your overall mental health will improve.

Don't Let the Trolls Be in Control

As a father of 5 kids, the founder of several multi-million dollar businesses, and the husband to one incredible wife, I've found that the best time for me to write this book is between the hours of 3:00 AM and 6:00 AM every day. Most people are not up at this time and therefore I can be even more intentional about not letting distractions steal my schedule. Trolls are people that have opinions about everything, but never actually accomplish anything.

When I get up at 3:00 AM I find that the trolls are quiet, mainly because they will be asleep until noon. Out of my Oral Roberts University college dorm room, I started one of America's largest wedding entertainment companies (DJConnection.com, which I have since sold) while the other men I went to college with were pursuing intramural basketball championships and seeking ways to experience "good times."

Rather than doing what most college students do, Ryan was laser-focused on becoming the masterful singer / song-writer that he is now today.

I am not judging the guys I went to college with (or maybe I am), even though they definitely judged me, however, I am simply pointing out that while others were enjoying the "college life", I was simply and simultaneously choosing to trade-up my time cold-calling businesses in route to building one of America's largest wedding entertainment companies, instead of listening to their opinions.

While Others Were Discussing Dreams, I Was Turning Them Into Reality. While most of the guys living in the dormitories were doing what college students do, wasting time and chasing girls, I spent my time branding, marketing and staffing my new business. For some reason, they always felt free to tell me their opinions about how I was making bad decisions. Ironic isn't it?

While I was on my grind, just down the hall from me, on the same floor (wing) of the dormitory, the now Grammy-award winning singer-songwriter, hit TV producer of NBC's Songland and the front man for OneRepublic, Ryan Tedder, was also grinding away and making the necessary trade-ups. Rather than doing what most college students do, Ryan was laser-focused on becoming the masterful singer / song-writer that he is now today.

In order for you to be successful, you will have to trade-up what others think about you...

While the vast majority of the men attending Oral Roberts University were enjoying "their college experience" Ryan was recording demos, mastering the guitar, practicing his vocals and producing melodic magic in his dorm room. In order for you to be successful, you will have to trade-up what others think about you, and be willing to do the actions needed to be successful, instead of listening to the opinions of trolls. If you listen to them, then you will end up where they are going.

Smartphone Fasting - The Power of Weekly Digital Detoxing

Today, staying super focused on the pursuit of your highest and best use is harder than ever before because we now live in this 24/7 digitally connected world.

However, I want YOU to know that I turn my phone off EVERY DAY when I come home and EVERY weekend between the hours of Friday at 5 PM and Monday at 6 AM. Why? Because, all weekend, and even as I write the pages of this book, I will receive an endless bombardment of employee wins, employee issues, customer wins, customer complaints, podcast lovers, podcast haters, and the updates from family members that frankly do not matter to me.

A few weeks ago I was told by a member of my family that another member of my family was getting divorced. I want you to know that I didn't care. In fact, because I live 100% of my life off of social media, I didn't even know about the drama that was being created as a result of their decision to be unfaithful to each other in the context of marriage.

I have specific times daily that I fast my smartphone.

Having personally helped hundreds of business owners and having spoken to thousands and thousands of people at speaking events all across this great country, I can tell you that the vast majority of people on the planet want to earn both time and financial freedom. Yet, the vast majority of people have allowed themselves to be too distracted to ever do so. However, this can change starting NOW. If you want to earn both time and financial freedom, then you must be willing to make those trade-ups that often are both obvious and difficult to make. What people will you not call back?

Whose emails will you choose to not respond to? What social media posts will you not look at? What frustrated client will you choose not to call back? What former employee will you choose to not respond to? What TV shows will you not watch? What smartphone app will you not use? What soccer games are you willing to miss? What weddings will you not attend?

NOTABLE QUOTABLE

"Always missing people that I shouldn't be missing. Sometimes you gotta burn some bridges just to create some distance."

GNASH

(Chart-topping songwriter and singer of the song, "I Hate U, I Love U.")

One of the best ways to start making these changes is to schedule time to disconnect. I recommend, at minimum, a weekly time where you fast your smartphone.

This means that for a specific amount of time, you turn off your device and put it in a place where you will not be able to quickly access it. As I mentioned above, I have specific times daily that I fast my smartphone. As you are starting out, start with 1x per week and increase your fasting amount over time.

Traction is what allows you to grip to the proven path.

F.O.C.U.S. on Traction Producing Activities

Traction is what allows you to grip to the proven path. As you diligently begin to implement the things I am teaching you, you will see that your traction will increase and you will start to experience exponential growth. I have been recording my podcast, The *Thrivetime Show, Business School Without the B.S.*, for many years now. Success requires trade-ups and super success requires making MASSIVE trade-ups that allow us to build traction. As of the very moment that I am writing these words, I have personally recorded 1,741 podcasts, each of which took me a minimum of over 3 hours to produce and prepare for.

Successful people don't focus on instant gratification, they F.O.C.U.S. (Focus On Core actions Until Successful).

This means that I have invested a minimum of 5,223 hours (130.5 40-hour work weeks) into the recording and producing of those chart-topping entrepreneurial interviews with the likes of Seth Godin, John Maxwell, Wolfgang Puck and other household names. In order to record those shows, I had to make trade-ups. I had to choose to be diligent and record consistently, even before I was able to get big names on the show. I had to F.O.C.U.S. (Focus On Core actions Until Successful). So, the question I would have for you is this, what do you want and what trade-ups are you willing to actually make in order to achieve those results? You need to start doing the necessary traction producing activities now so that you can create the momentum needed to get to your goals.

"Someday" is not a day in your calendar.

This will require you to make trade-ups today that will get you to your goals down the road. Successful people don't focus on instant gratification, they F.O.C.U.S. (Focus On Core actions Until Successful). They are diligent doers that consistently implement the proven actions and systems day after day until they get the results they want.

Start Now, Some Day Is Not in Your Calendar

Life is Not a Dress Rehearsal. I love my job, the businesses I coach, the businesses I own, the people I work with, the woman I've been married to for 18 consecutive years (Vanessa) and my incredible five kids. However, according to Gallup, well over 70% of Americans do not like their jobs, and according to Psychology Today, well over 70% of Americans don't like their spouses either. That is so sad to me because YOU only have one shot (that I know about) to play this game called life. Thus, you need to get started today! None of us know how many days we will be privileged to have on this planet. Someday is not a day in your calendar.

You need to start today!

CHAPTER 1

DETERMINE YOUR F6 GOALS TODAY OR YOU ARE F'D

(THE "F" STANDS FOR "unFOCUSED." OBVIOUSLY)

As the rapper, Eminem, said in his wildly famous song "One Shot", "You better lose yourself in the music, the moment you own it, you better never let it go. You only get one shot, do not miss your chance to blow, this opportunity comes once in a lifetime." We only have one opportunity and one shot at this game called life and we are all busy. However, none of us are too busy to achieve success. I know your schedule may seem overwhelming, but you can get things under control. As the co-founder of 5 kids (which means that "we got busy"), the founder of multiple multi-dollar businesses and the host of a podcast (*The Thrivetime Show*) that releases 9 episodes per week, I can assure you that despite how busy you think you are, you DO HAVE THE TIME to achieve your goals.

Puff, Steve, Jeff, Bill, Larry and John had the same 24 hours per day I have, yet they are somehow investing those 24 hours more productively than I am... What are they not doing that I'm doing?

However, first and foremost, in order to achieve success and to begin to trade-up to living our best life, we must take the time needed to write down our goals for the next 12 months. If we don't, we will magically drift through yet another year of intentions, "I-did-my-best" and secret despair as the crowd cheers and we try to hold back our tears when watching Ryan Seacrest on December 31st announcing the dropping of the ball on this year's edition of Dick Clark's Rockin' Eve!

If you and I have no MAJOR PURPOSE, we are going to drift towards certain failure by default. Mentally marinate on that for a second. If you and I have no MAJOR PURPOSE, we are going to drift towards certain failure by default. When I was 18 years old, I remember sitting in my Oral Roberts University dorm room. It was located on the fourth floor of the EMR dormitory. I was eating Raman noodles while reading Newsweek and obsessing on the idea that Steve Jobs, Puff Daddy (now known as Diddy), Steve Case (the founder of AOL), Jeff Bezos (the founder of Amazon.com), Bill Gates (the founder of Microsoft), Larry Ellison (the founder of Oracle) and John Chambers (the founder of Cisco) all had just 24 hours in every day just like me.

Right now, you must get out a pen (I know that's old school) and write down your goals.

I'm not sure why I became obsessed with this idea, but I literally became obsessed with time management without knowing it. I vividly remember having the thought: Puff, Steve, Jeff, Bill, Larry and John had the same 24 hours per day I have, yet they are somehow investing those 24 hours more productively than I am…What are they not doing that I'm doing? What did they do at the age of 18 that I'm not doing now? I wonder if I did exactly what they did on a daily basis if I too would achieve massive success?

From that moment on, I began to make trade-ups so that I could intentionally design each and every day of my life. However, at the young age of 18, I didn't realize that life consisted of more than just the achievement of my love interest and financial success. Thus, by default, nearly 100% of my to-do-list was occupied with just 2 things.

…the vast majority of people do not have clearly defined goals.

I was going to date and marry Vanessa Moore, that cheerleader with the curly hair, sage mind and that incredible behind. I was going to marry her and have 5 kids. I was going to build DJConnection.com into a multi-million dollar business, even if it killed me in the process.

Vanessa Clark is my wife and the love of my life.

Now, at the age of 38, while writing this at 3:38 AM on Father's Day 2019, I can tell you that I did marry my "Dream Woman" Vanessa Moore, now Vanessa Clark. I can tell you that we did produce those 5 incredible kids (Havana, Aubrey, Angelina, Laya and Scarlett) and I can tell you that together, Vanessa and I did grow DJConnection.com into a multi-million dollar business. I can also tell you that it's very important that you and I intentionally schedule time for the achievement of all 6 of the F6 areas of your life or by default, our dreams will not become a reality. Right now, you must get out a pen (I know that's old school) and write down your goals.

Having invested over a decade of my life coaching wonderful clients at workshops, conferences, and during one-on-one coaching sessions, I can assure you that the vast majority of people do not have clearly defined goals. However, because I am of the belief that you have both the mental capacity and tenacity needed to begin creating the momentum filled life that we all want, I want to challenge you to define your Specific, Measurable, Achievable, Realistic and Time-sensitive (S.M.A.R.T) goals for the following areas of your life:

What are your faith goals for the next 12 months?

. . . .

What are your family goals for the next 12 months?

. . . .

What are your financial goals for the next 12 months?

. . . .

What are your fitness goals for the next 12 months?

. . . .

What are your friendship goals for the next 12 months?

. . . .

What are your fun goals for the next 12 months?

. . . .

Some examples of S.M.A.R.T. goals may be:

EXAMPLE #1: I want to reach page one in Google search engine results for my industry in the next 12 months. In order to make it happen I am going to: Record and transcribe a keyword rich and relevant 15-minute podcast every day and gather 1 objective Google review from a real happy client everyday.

EXAMPLE #2: I am going to save $400 per month during the next 12 months by automating the saving of 5% of my income tomorrow with the HR department.

Examples of non S.M.A.R.T. goals would be:

EXAMPLE #1: I want to live a better and more inspirational life that is filled with passion.

EXAMPLE #2: I want to become more authentic with my inner self this year.

As you pursue the success that you seek, you will quickly discover that the people whom you choose to surround yourself with on a daily basis will directly magnify or minimize the amount of success that you are able to achieve. As an example, when I was growing DJConnection. com, I quickly discovered that the men and women who were in charge of the food and beverage departments of the massive hotels (The Dallas Hilton Anatole Hotel and the Tulsa Mayo Hotel, etc.) were ultimately the people who soon-to-be brides would ask for a recommendation from when it came time to booking their wedding DJ.

I traded-up my time so that I could know my specific S.M.A.R.T. F6 goals.

Thus, back-in-the-day, when I still owned DJConnection.com I would schedule a time to meet with these influencers and build relationships with them, and thus our DJ Empire quickly expanded both its power and influence. However, as a result of choosing to invest time with these influential wedding vendors, I was forced to no longer invest my time into dysfunctional pursuits like meeting with wedding vendor startups (florists, caterers, videographers, etc.) who were always trying to pick my brain about how to build the biggest and best wedding vendor business possible. The main reason I was able to focus my attention on the revenue creating relationships was because I traded-up my time so that I could know my specific S.M.A.R.T. F6 goals. This empowered me to make good decisions and avoid drifting. Proverbs 29:18 KJV says, "Where there is no vision, the people perish…" As I read this, I understand that my F6 goals are my "vision". Without them, my dreams will perish. So will yours.

Make your F6 goals today. Don't skip this step. It is foundational for what comes next.

CHAPTER 2

DESIGN YOUR DAYS

(THE ART OF MORNING META MAPPING)

I invest the time needed to plan my day and organize my one to-do-list by utilizing my calendar, each and every morning...

Knowing my F6 goals allows me to intentionally design my day. Everyday (as of the time I am writing this, June of 2019) I choose to wake up at 3:00 AM. Do I want to wake up at 3:00 AM? No. Why do I do it? I choose to wake up at 3:00 AM every day now because I have my eyes on the achievement of the goals I have set for myself in the areas of: Faith, Family, Finances, Fitness, Friendship and Fun. Thus, I trade-up sleep, currently go to bed at 9 PM, and I wake up at 3 AM. When I wake up at 3 AM, guess who is calling me? No one. Guess who is interrupting me? No one. Guess what distractions are standing in the way of me completing my action items at 3 AM? No one. Thus, I get almost a full 4 hours done before most people even wake up. So, what am I doing with my time between the hours of 3 AM and 7 AM?

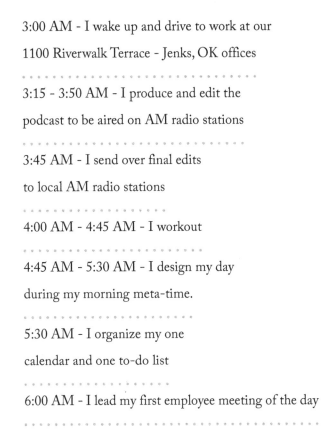

3:00 AM - I wake up and drive to work at our
1100 Riverwalk Terrace - Jenks, OK offices

3:15 - 3:50 AM - I produce and edit the
podcast to be aired on AM radio stations

3:45 AM - I send over final edits
to local AM radio stations

4:00 AM - 4:45 AM - I workout

4:45 AM - 5:30 AM - I design my day
during my morning meta-time.

5:30 AM - I organize my one
calendar and one to-do list

6:00 AM - I lead my first employee meeting of the day

So What's the Secret to My Success? My meta time is what I want to dive into. Meta time is the time I set aside to plan my day, ensuring that I am doing what really needs done. This helps me make sure I am trading-up my time for the right actions. I invest the time needed to plan my day and organize my one to-do-list by utilizing my calendar, each and every morning, because I recognize that we only live once and that only what gets scheduled gets done by default. Whether it's attending my daughter's 8th grade graduation or closing a massive business deal, I have learned that if you and I are not intentional about scheduling time for what matters, our schedules will magically fill themselves with things that don't matter, obligations and perpetual distractions (Chamber of Commerce Events, mindless business networking groups, home fellowship groups attended by people that you don't like, being volunteered to bring chips and carbonated beverages for the soccer team, etc.).

Lets go ahead and practice the art of designing your day. Take a couple minutes and go through the questions below. Do not leave any time blank. Tell every moment of your Monday where it should go.

MONDAY:

4:00 AM - What activities do you want to do (need to do)?

_____

5:00 AM - What activities do you want to do (need to do)?

_____

6:00 AM - What activities do you want to do (need to do)?

_____

7:00 AM - What activities do you want to do (need to do)?

_____

8:00 AM - What activities do you want to do (need to do)?

_____

9:00 AM - What activities do you want to do (need to do)?

_____

10:00 AM - What activities do you want to do (need to do)?

_____

11:00 AM - What activities do you want to do (need to do)?

_____

12:00 PM - What activities do you want to do (need to do)?

_____

1:00 PM - What activities do you want to do (need to do)?

_____

2:00 PM - What activities do you want to do (need to do)?

_____

3:00 PM - What activities do you want to do (need to do)?

_____

4:00 PM - What activities do you want to do (need to do)?

_____

5:00 PM - What activities do you want to do (need to do)?

_____

6:00 PM - What activities do you want to do (need to do)?z

_____

7:00 PM - What activities do you want to do (need to do)?

_____

8:00 PM - What activities do you want to do (need to do)?

_____

9:00 PM - What activities do you want to do (need to do)?

_____

≈≈≈

****Remember, what gets scheduled gets done. Don't skip the activity above!****

≈≈≈

Now that you have designed your magical Monday what distractions will prevent you from living out that Monday?

_____

In order to make that distraction free Monday a reality, what changes do you have to make in order to make your perfect Monday possible?

_____

_____

_____

Now, go through this process for every day of your week. Once you have done this, add these items to your calendar. If you don't have a calendar, get one.

Where Did the Time Go?

Now that you have traded-up your time to plan your days, remember that you are beginning to implement the actions of super successful people. Oprah, Warren Buffett, Sarah Blakely, Lebron James, Ellen, and you all have the exact same number of hours available in a day to gain traction in this modern world of perpetual distraction where the average person is now listening to, watching, reading or generally interacting with media over 11 hours per day according to Nielsen? They are planning their days, and now, so are you. I am of the opinion that, regardless of what is politically correct or not, people do judge you based upon what you actually do and not based upon what you could do or have the potential to do. If you actually did the assignment of planning your days, then I applaud you. Now, your next vital step is to get up early everyday, go over your plan/schedule for the day and actually follow the plan.

FUN FACT:
When Oprah is hosting a TV show, acting in a movie, delivering a keynote address or receiving an award she is not simultaneously texting, updating her social media account and filming the event that is actually happening while at the event.

In order for you to to even hope to begin to live a life with as much intentionality as Oprah, Steve Jobs, and all of the other successful people that we have talked about, you must plan your days. You must be intentional about making the Trade-ups needed to plan your day and actually stick to the plan.

Here is the summary of meta time:

1. Know your goals

2. Create a calendar where you keep your daily plan for working towards those goals.

3. Get up early and go over the plan.

4. Print out your calendar and to-do list

5. Use your calendar and to-do list throughout the day. Take them with you everywhere you go.

CHAPTER 3

WHAT GETS SCHEDULED GETS DONE

I invest the time needed to plan my day and organize my one to-do-list by utilizing my calendar, each and every morning...

Now that you are armed with your F6 goals, you have made a daily plan, you are starting to learn how to utilize a calendar, wake up early every morning, and get yourself a physical to-do list, you need to set time aside to actually be working towards these goals on a consistent basis. Unless you have been able to dramatically alter your schedule since you finished reading that last page, I would imagine that you are finding yourself at a place where you now have a better idea about where and who you should be spending your time with.

Yet, the very thought of achieving the big goals that we have allowed to drift out of focus in our lives can feel overwhelming if you've never actually first sat down to determine where you are currently spending your time. We know that yesterday has come and gone, but where did your time actually go?

Thus, we have to get to work auditing yesterday. What did you do yesterday? Think hard about it and fill out the following worksheet honestly so that we can get a better handle on how you have been choosing to invest your time.

Fact

"Young adults 18-34 spend 43% of their time consuming media on digital platforms. Almost a third of their time spent with media (29%) comes from apps/web on a smartphone—the most of any measured generation."

https://www.nielsen.com/us/en/insights/news/2018/
time-flies-us-adults-now-spend-nearly-half-
a-day-interacting-with-media.print.html

5:00 AM - What did you do?

_____

5:30 AM - What did you do?

_____

6:00 AM - What did you do?

_____

6:30 AM - What did you do?

_____

7:00 AM - What did you do?

_____

7:30 AM - What did you do?

_____

8:00 AM - What did you do?

_____

8:30 AM - What did you do

_____

9:00 AM - What did you do?

_____

9:30 AM - What did you do?

_____

10:00 AM - What did you do?

_____

10:30 AM - What did you do?

_____

11:00 AM - What did you do?

_____

11:30 AM - What did you do?

_____

12:00 PM - What did you do?

_____

12:30 PM - What did you do?

_____

1:00 PM - What did you do?

_____

1:30 PM - What did you do?

_____

2:00 PM - What did you do?

_____

2:30 PM - What did you do?

_____

3:00 PM - What did you do?

_____

3:30 PM - What did you do?

_____

4:00 PM - What did you do?

_____

4:30 PM - What did you do?

_____

5:00 PM - What did you do?

_____

Now that you have taken the time needed to account for where and how
you spent your time yesterday, it's important that you take out a pen and
cross out the activities that are not helping you to move closer towards
the achievement of your goals. This is the tough part for most people,
because when you first begin to become intentional with how you invest
your time, you are going to quickly realize that you are investing both
your time and energy in activities and people that are an epic waste

of time. I know that sounds harsh, but consider the following notable quotables before getting mad at me. Then you can get mad at me...

NOTABLE QUOTABLE

"Walk with the wise and become wise, for a companion of fools suffers harm."

PROVERBS 13:20

(From that controversial book known as The Bible)

NOTABLE QUOTABLE

"You are the average of the five people you most associate with."

TIM FERRISS

(*The New York Times* best-selling author of The 4-Hour Workweek, The 4-Hour Body, The 4-Hour Chef, Tools of Titans and Tribe of Mentors and an angel investor in Facebook, Twitter, Evernote and Uber)

NOTABLE QUOTABLE

"Surround yourself with only people who are going to lift you higher."

OPRAH WINFREY

(The iconic media executive, actress, talk show host, television and philanthropist who became the first African American billionaire in 2003)

For years, as a natural empathetic coach and teacher I chose to waste

I encourage you to make a list of the people that are holding you back with their chronic negativity

hundreds of hours of one-on-one time that I can never get back, coaching people up who struggled with such difficult concepts as:

- How do I show up to work on time?
- How to not impregnate someone I just met who is currently married?
- How to stay drug free for 1 week in a row?
- How do I stay faithful to my wife (how do I keep my pants on)?
- How do I stop showing up to work drunk?
- How do I stop trying to steal the systems, processes, and everything you have ever built at DJConnection.com while still remaining friends with your current friends?

Now my life is very different because no one in my inner circle is coming to me to solve their life dramas related to:

- Chronic lateness
- Baby creation with someone they just met
- Staying drug free
- Cheating on their wife
- Being day-drunk
- Attempting to screw me

You've known for years, deep inside, that certain people are holding you back with their dream killing negativity and their endless drama, but you don't want to block them out of your life because you care about them. But, it's now time to decide once and for all.

Are you going to invest your entire life being a person who always bails out your dysfunctional family and friends in their time of need, or are you going to be a person who achieves your dreams because you refuse to wear the ankle weights known as "chronically dysfunctional people"?

I encourage you to make a list of the people that are holding you back with their chronic negativity, dysfunction and doubts. Who are you going to commit to stop investing your time with starting tomorrow?

Person #1 - This person is holding you back by creating endless emergencies and drama in your life:

- Why are they holding you back?

_____

- Have you asked them to stop their dysfunctional behavior?

_____

Person #2 - This person is holding you back by creating endless emergencies and drama in your life:

- Why are they holding you back?

_____

- Have you asked them to stop their dysfunctional behavior?

_____

Person #3 - This person is holding you back by creating endless emergencies and drama in your life:

- Why are they holding you back?

  _____

- Have you asked them to stop their dysfunctional behavior?

  _____

Person #4 - This person is holding you back by creating endless emergencies and drama in your life:

- Why are they holding you back?

  _____

- Have you asked them to stop their dysfunctional behavior?

  _____

If you have more than 4 people that are holding you back, I am sorry and thus I have created extra space for you to list who they are and what you are going to do about it.

_____

_____

_____

_____

STORY TIME:

Now just to provide a little context for the previous exercise, the first company that I started out of my college dorm room was DJConnection.com, which became one of America's largest wedding entertainment services. Before I sold the company I was surrounded by well-meaning disc jockeys for the vast majority of my waking hours. I'm sure that the DJs that they hire today are much better and different from the men that I used to hire, but on a daily basis I was surrounded by dead-beat fathers and men who would ask me if I was willing to pay them cash so that they could avoid paying child support to their baby's mama. On a daily basis, I was surrounded by men in their 30s and 40s whose top goal and priority was to see if I would be willing to assign them to DJ at certain clubs so that they could be at the elite venues where "the hot girls" were at. My friend, I cannot possibly describe how many idiots, degenerates and scammers were in my life at the time I first started DJConnection.com. After I sold the business, one of the former employees kept reaching out to me with his business and life questions. Before selling the business I gave this

employee the opportunity to join me at one of my existing businesses, but he declined. However, he still viewed me as his mentor. Thus, even though he was no longer my employee he kept asking me for advice and mentorship on a daily basis because "his current boss couldn't help him." Although this might sound harsh, I value spending time with my own family more than I value responding to the questions, texts and calls from former employees who willingly and intentionally chose to not stay on my payroll. I called him and let him know that since he was no longer on my team as a result of his choice to not join my team, he no longer had my ear and that I would no longer be calling him back, texting him back or responding to him in any other way. Because I have sold multiple businesses, imagine how terrible my life would be if I had chosen to continually respond to the countless emails, texts, and calls for advice I receive on a daily basis from my former teammates. You must trade-up the people in your life who are taking you away from pursuing your F6 goals.

Next, you must figure out, when will you invest the time needed to take the actions that are required for you to achieve your goals in the F6 areas of your life? Here are several examples of some of my F6 goals and some questions to help you on this journey.

Faith

Example - I listen to TD Jakes sermons on Youtube each and every morning on Youtube because I have found that I have to mentally reset and to feed myself spiritually every morning to remain positive while managing the day-to-day and often soul-sucking tasks involved in operating successful businesses.

- What Day Each Week Will You Pursue Your Faith Goals?

  _____

- What Time? _____

Family

Example - My wife and kids matter to me very much and thus I schedule time to spend with them. However, certain members of my extended family have proven themselves time-and-time again to be dysfunctional, dramatic and actually dangerous, thus I do not schedule time to spend with these individuals.

- What Day Each Week Will You Pursue Your Faith Goals?

  _____

- What Time?

  _____

Finances

Example - I know specifically how much money my wife and I need to live each and every year based upon the lifestyle that we choose to live and our lifestyle includes:

- We will live on 15 acres of land (soon to be 37 additional acres).

- I enjoy planting trees every weekend (preferably pine trees).

- 3 of our daughters are enrolled in private cheer lessons.

- Our kids are enrolled in private weekly piano and drum lessons.

- We prefer home-schooling and private schooling our kids.

- We have 13 cats (currently) that we must feed and care for.

- We have 30 + chickens (preferably silkie chickens) and 1 domesticated turkey named "Thom" that we must feed and care for.

- We have one "Man Cave" that requires a weekly purchase of something from Guitar Center, Hobby Lobby and Atwoods.

- We love to have family and friends over every Sunday (preferably at 6 PM).

At all times I must be learning, earning or burning.

- What Day Each Week Will You Pursue Your Financial Goals?

  _____

- What Time?

  _____

Fitness

Example - I don't want to die early as a result of obesity, but I don't have plans on competing in a fitness challenge that requires me to tan my body any time soon.

What Day Each Week Will You Pursue Your Fitness Goals?

_____

What Time?

_____

Friendship

Example - I firmly believe that our network will determine our net worth and that you and I will become the average of the five people that we spend the most time with. Thus, I refuse to suffer fools anymore and to spend my time with people that are going nowhere and want company.

What Day Each Week Will You Pursue Your Friendship Goals?

_____

What Time?

_____

NOTABLE QUOTABLE

"The secret of happiness is minimizing the amount of time you spend with people you don't choose to be with. This is just math!"

PHIL LIBIN
(The former CEO of Evernote)

Fun

Example - My wife is my life and she determines what fun things that we need to do next. By default I am a hard-working grinder who needs constant reminders that "we will be dead soon so we should probably schedule some time to enjoy the fruits of our efforts." Vanessa is the person who is 100% responsible for deciding what trips, cruises, vacations or fun things that we do as a family.

What Day Each Week Will You Pursue Your Fun Goals?

_____

What Time?

_____

In order for you to become hard-wired for success and for your new default setting to be the achievement of success you must make sure that the action steps that you are taking on a daily basis are actually getting you closer to the achievement of your F6 goals and are not causing you to drift further and further away from the ideal schedule and lifestyle that you want. This requires you to have the courage to trade-up what you feel like doing for what you need to do. You must create rocks in your schedule.

> **If I didn't have the combination of my calendar (with the rocks) and my to-do list (sand) physically in hand with me everywhere I go throughout the day, then I would not stay focused on the things that must get done to achieve my F6 goals.**

A rock is an unmovable object in your schedule that helps you set standards and that you stay committed to come hell or high water. As you go over the plan for your day and ensure that your rocks are properly scheduled, you will be able to fill the rest of the time with sand. Sand represents the essential, to-do, items that must get done, but that don't require a specific time of day to accomplish. If a meeting gets finished early and I have some extra time, I am usually able to knock a few of my sand items off of my to-do list. If I didn't have the combination of my calendar (with the rocks) and my to-do list (sand) physically in hand with me everywhere I go throughout the day, then I would not stay focused on the things that must get done to achieve my F6 goals. Having these items ensures that I am constantly trading-up my time for the right things.

CHAPTER 4

YOU MUST SAY NO TO GROW

(DEFINING YOUR DIGITAL BOUNDARIES)

Most people on their deathbed would agree that time is our most precious asset because we can't make more of it. Yet, by default, without being intentional, it can be very easy to allow yourself to have your time stolen by the endless "time robbers" swirling all around us. If we are not careful we can spend vast portions of our day being interrupted by "got-a-minute meetings," "chain emails," "Chuck Norris jokes" on social media and the formality-filled bureaucracy buffets known as the homeowner's association meetings.

Fact

New Study Shows You're Wasting 21.8 hours a Week - The business leaders we polled spent 6.8 hours per week on low value business activities that they could easily have paid somebody else $50/hour or less to handle for them. They wasted 3.9 hours each week indulging in what we might call escapist "mental health breaks" --streaming YouTube videos and checking social media. They wasted 3.4 hours a week handling low-value emails and 3.2 hours a week dealing with low-value interruptions that easily could have been handled by somebody else on staff. They spent 1.8 hours a week handling low-value requests from co-workers and another 1.8 hours a week putting out preventable fires. Finally, they spent an average of 1 hour each week sitting in completely non-productive or wasteful meetings. Total that up and we're looking at 21.8 wasted hours each week -- hours that are going up in smoke while you're doing things that contribute little to no value to your company.

https://www.inc.com/david-finkel/new-study-shows-youre-wasting-218-hours-a-week.html

I am often asked by listeners of our Thrivetime Show podcast if they can shadow me for a day or two so that they can see how I actually organize my day, lead teams, manage people, and deal with the burning fires, while still being the husband to 1 and father of 5 kids. I don't mind, and I know that allowing people to shadow me provides many entrepreneurs with the experiential learning event that most of us need to really master new skills so I usually allow two people to shadow me each month and this is essentially what the shadows are in for:

5:00 - Meta time - This is the time I invest every morning in organizing my schedule, and planning out my day's to do list.

. . . .

6:00 - Staff meeting #1 - This is the first staff meeting is where I invest my time to answer the questions that my coach's have from their clients as it relates to implementing the customized business plan that I have personally designed for them.

. . . .

7:00 - Elephant In The Room Manager's Meeting - This is the manager's only meeting for Elephant In The Room where we celebrate wins of the week, and follow up on the revenue producing activities and the key performance indicators.

. . . .

8:00 - All Staff Meeting - This is the one meeting per week where we invest the time to celebrate the "wins of the week" and to provide on-going practical life skill training for the various members of our team.

. . . .

9:00 - Coaching Session with Client #1

10:00 - Coaching Session with Client #2

11:00 - Meeting with the Tip Top
K9 Franchise ownership team

12:00 - Coaching Session with Client #3

1:00 - Drive to the Man-Cave Studios at Camp
Clark and Chicken Palace at the Lampoon Lagoon

2:00 - 4:30 - Record the Podcast

4:30 - Chase my wife and kids around

Fact

"50% of teens feel they are addicted
to their mobile devices."

CNN

(Smartphone Addiction Could Be Changing Your
Brain - https://www.cnn.com/2016/05/03/health/
teens-cell-phone-addiction-parents/index.html)

As I get prepared to walk the person shadowing me out and to give that person a "brofessional hug," I often ask those that shadow what they learned, or what insights they gained as a result of shadowing me and they typically say something to the effect of:

1. "I can't believe how much you got done today and that you didn't even use a smartphone 90% of the day."

2. "When do you typically go out and eat lunch?"

3. "Do you really always wear the same thing every day?"

4. "It's crazy how you've designed your life so that

   you never have to leave your office."

5. "I can't believe that you use a printed paper to-do list and calendar."

6. "It's crazy that you didn't spend any of your time on email."

NOTABLE QUOTABLE

"The secret of your success is determined by your daily agenda."

JOHN MAXWELL

(The multiple time *New York Times* best-selling author and the author of *The 21 Irrefutable Laws of Leadership*)

...You will end up quickly running off course if you are not made to remain focused on the achievement of your F6 goals.

In order to achieve your goals and to live your best life now you must become very comfortable with living as though you are wearing a massive "Do Not Disturb" sign the vast majority of the time. When you stay at a hotel, most hotels provide you with a sign that you can hang on your hotel room door knob that reads, "Do Not Disturb" so that the housekeeping service does not interrupt you as you sleep, work on projects, etc. In order to achieve massive success you must act as though you are wearing a "Do Not Disturb" sign around your neck when you are working on your proactive projects and the pursuit of your goals otherwise you will find yourself being always interrupted by people (nearly everybody on the planet) who do not understand or care whether you achieve your dreams or not.

Having worked with and personally coached hundreds of business owners, I want to also encourage you that you also must become a grinder who is wearing blinders. Just like the fast-moving horses that have peripheral vision, you will end up quickly running off course if you are not made to remain focused on the achievement of your F6 goals. In this world of endless distraction you must learn how to let go of the Fear Of Missing Out (F.O.M.O.) experienced by most people who spend their days and nights worrying about whether they are missing something that just happened on social media or what is in their email inboxes.

Fact

"86% of Americans say they check their email and social media accounts "constantly," and that it's really stressing them out."

-https://www.businessinsider.com/what-your-smartphone-is-doing-to-your-brain-and-it-isnt-good-2018-3

Do you remember what happened to you last year on Facebook on your birthday? People you know well and that girl that you used to date back in third grade all took time out of their schedule to wish you a happy birthday, and then you took the time needed to sincerely thank each and every Facebook birthday well-wisher for taking the time needed to wish you a happy birthday.

Essentially, nothing got done, but you stayed super busy all day doing mindless tasks that did not help you to get closer to the achievement of your life goals. Thus, at the end of the day you may have felt empty and depressed because you didn't get anything done, yet you stayed super busy. In today's always connected digital age you and I must become more intentional about what activities we will engage in during our days.

Fact

"Twice as many heavy users of electronic devices are unhappy, depressed or distressed as light users."

- https://time.com/5555737/smartphone-mental-health-teens/

As an example, you don't always need to return that call to the people that call you for the exact same reason that we don't call the companies who relentlessly mail us marketing print pieces to let them know that we will be declining their offer for 30% off of their super-duper deluxe pizza. With today's digital technology and the constant bombardment of communication that we all receive on a daily basis from our email, Facebook accounts, Google My Business review updates, Instagram accounts, Linkedin accounts, Twitter accounts, text messages, voicemail, Youtube accounts, etc. you simply have to learn to say "no" to grow.

Successful people have taught themselves the art of F.O.C.U.S. Successful people have learned how to Focus On Core Tasks Until Success.

In fact if you want to achieve your goals you need to learn to make "no" your default answer for almost all interruptions, thus you can save your best for when you say "yes." Remember this rule. You must learn to say "no" to everything unless it's a "hell yes" if you ever want to achieve your best. As the word "no" becomes your default response, you will find that the "yes's" you are trading-up for are much better than the things you are declining to be a part of.

Successful people have taught themselves the art of F.O.C.U.S. Successful people have learned how to Focus On Core Tasks Until Success. So what are the practical steps that you need to take to say "no" to every distraction that the world has to offer?

If you are going to achieve success during your lifetime with your career you must begin to act like a professional and that will require you to turn off your smartphone and your push notifications for 80% to 90% of your work day.

Step 1

Turn your phone onto "airplane mode" or leave it in your car unless you need it. What?! What if the world ends!? What if somebody needs to reach you!? Well, I have thought about the trade-ups and I am 100% convinced that turning your phone onto "airplane mode" 80% to 90% of the time is the powerful step that you must learn to take if you want to achieve massive success. In fact, as I am writing this very page of this book, my phone is turned onto "Airplane mode" and it has been left inside my Hummer. Why? Because I don't want to be reached and I want 100% of my focus to be on writing the best book I can possibly deliver so you can gain traction in this world of perpetual distraction.

Step 2

Turn your push notifications off on your phone. For me and you it's not healthy to be updated 24/7 about what email you just received, what text message you just received, who just left you a good or bad review on your Google My Business Account, what your aunt thinks about President Trump on Facebook and what new files were just added to your Dropbox file storage account.

Step 3

Commit to not worry about what happens when you are unreachable. As I am writing this, I am unreachable by hundreds of my employees and hundreds of our valued clients. Why? Because it's impossible to create an environment where work matters while being constantly interrupted. How horrible would professional basketball be to watch if the players kept their cell phones on them during the games and called occasional random timeouts to tuck their kids into bed over the phone, to respond to the negative comments from fans on their social media accounts and to take the occasional call from their spouses. If you are going to achieve success during your lifetime with your career you must begin to act like a professional and that will require you to turn off your smartphone and your push notifications for 80% to 90% of your work day.

Fact

"Endocrinologist Robert Lustig tells *Business Insider* that notifications from our phones are training our brains to be in a near constant state of stress and fear by establishing a stress-fear memory pathway. And such a state means that the prefrontal

> cortex, the part of our brains that normally deals with some of our highest-order cognitive functioning, goes completely haywire, and basically shuts down."
> -https://www.businessinsider.com/what-your-smartphone-is-doing-to-your-brain-and-it-isnt-good-2018-3

Saying "No" for a Season Isn't an Act of Treason (or is it?) Having interviewed countless multi-millionaires and super success stories (like Wolfgang Puck, John Maxwell and Seth Godin) on our *Thrivetime Show* podcast, I can tell you that they have all had to learn to say "No" to countless good things and opportunities in their lives in order to free up the time they needed to pursue their game-changing ideas.

This is the essence of Trade-ups. You must say "No" to things so that you can trade-up and say "Yes" to the best things.

You Must Learn to Say "No". If you want to take your career, your marriage, your family or any aspect of your life to the next level you are going to have to become masterful at tactfully, nicely and often bluntly saying "No." However, the first time that you tell your friend from college that you will not be attending their kid's graduation (because you have to finish a book proposal) get ready for people to get mad at you. The first time that you tell your Chamber of Commerce representative that you don't want to renew your membership because you "no longer value networking" get ready for somebody to get mad at you.

> A "rock" is an unmovable object in
> your schedule that helps you set
> standards and that you stay committed
> to come hell or high water.

When you decide to entirely stop responding to all social media comments and messages get ready for a member of your family or a friend to get mad at you. Once you ascend to the "NEXT LEVEL NARNIA" that I call my life and you let people know that you no longer respond to email, prepare yourself for the hate parade to be producing massive volume in your life. However, I would encourage you to know that once people start complaining about your perpetual unavailability, you will know that you are on the right path. You only live once, and as you fully commit to a diet or philosophy of any kind that has been proven to work, you must prepare yourself for people to not be happy with you. Once YOU fully commit to eating only organic meat and vegetables in route to becoming a slimmer version of yourself get ready for others to get frustrated that you will not be eating the carbohydrates, the empty calories and the things that everybody else is eating.

As pastor Craig Groeschel says, "I don't worry when people are complaining about me, I worry when they are not."

If you are standing for something, chasing after your goals, and sticking to the standards you set for your life, you are going to upset someone. This is a good thing. You are trading-up the opinions of others in order to stand for what you really want.

Let this fuel you to know that you are on the right path. Say "no" to grow and let all the haters go!

A rock is an unmovable object in your schedule that helps you set standards and that you stay committed to come hell or high water. As you go over the plan for your day and ensure that your rocks are properly scheduled, you will be able to fill the rest of the time with sand.

Sand represents the essential, to-do, items that must get done, but that don't require a specific time of day to accomplish. If a meeting gets finished early and I have some extra time, I am usually able to knock a few of my sand items off of my to-do list.

If I didn't have the combination of my calendar (with the rocks) and my to-do list (sand) physically in hand with me everywhere I go throughout the day, then I would not stay focused on the things that must get done to achieve my F6 goals. Having these items ensures that I am constantly trading-up my time for the right things.

CHAPTER 5

BEING PRESENT IS A PRESENT

(DON'T TEXT WHILE DRIVING, WORKING OR HAVING SEX)

Don't Allow Smartphones to Make You Dumb. According to studies published in *Psychology Today*, the average American is obsessed with their phone, which is why they check their phones 47 times per day according to *Inc Magazine*, and why the average humans is interrupted over 85 times per day, according to *Psychology Today*. Most people now live in a distraction filled digital dystopia and many people are literally dying from it. Don't believe me? Check these disturbing statistics:

"According to the US Centers for Disease Control and Prevention, mobile phone use is partially to blame for the distracted driving that kills an estimated nine people each day and injures more than 1,000."

SANDEE LAMOTTE - CNN
"Smartphone addiction could be changing your brain"

"Here's another disturbing stat: This tally seems to increase daily, but by one study's count, the typical smartphone user interacts with their phone around 85 times per day."

ANNA AKBARI PH.D. - *PSYCHOLOGY TODAY*
"Why Your Smartphone Is Destroying Your Life" -
Psychology Today - https://www.psychologytoday.
com/us/blog/startup-your-life/201801/why-
your-smartphone-is-destroying-your-life

"According to research cited in Forbes, the average office worker spends 2.5 hours a day reading and responding to an average of 200 emails, of which approximately 144 (mostly CCs and BCCs) aren't relevant to their job."

GEOFFREY JAMES - *INC. MAGAZINE*
*Tasks - Inc. Magazine "The Average Worker Spends 51%
of Each Workday on These 3 Unnecessary Tasks"* - https://
www.inc.com/geoffrey-james/the-average-worker-spends-
51-of-each-workday-on-these-3-unnecessary-tasks.html

"Research published by the University of Chicago found that even if cell phones are turned off, turned face down or put away their mere presence reduces people's cognitive capacity."

ABIGAIL HESS - CNBC

Research continually shows how distracting cell phones are—so some schools want to ban them
- CNBC - https://www.cnbc.com/2019/01/18/research-shows-that-cell-phones-distract-students--so-france-banned-them-in-school--.html#targetText=Research%20published%20by%20the%20University,presence%20reduces%20people's%20cognitive%20capacity.

"Since 1999, the number of drug overdose deaths has more than quadrupled. Deaths attributed to opioids were nearly six times greater in 2017 than they were in 1999."

LENNY BERNSTEIN - *WASHINGTON POST*

- U.S. life expectancy declines again, a dismal trend not seen since World War I - Washington Post -
-https://www.washingtonpost.com/national/health-science/us-life-expectancy-declines-again-a-dismal-trend-not-seen-since-world-war-i/2018/11/28/ae58bc8c-f28c-11e8-bc79-68604ed88993_story.html

NOTABLE QUOTABLE

"We need to re-create boundaries. When you carry a digital gadget that creates a virtual link to the office, you need to create a virtual boundary that didn't exist before."

DANIEL GOLEMAN

(The *New York Times* best-selling author of *Emotional Intelligence* and a recipient of the Career Achievement award for Excellence in the Media (1984) from the American Psychological Association)

Example #1

It's constant digital distraction caused by couples sitting physically together during dinner while they each spend the entire dinner messing with their phone. He's flipping through ESPN and FOXNews.com, she's responding to text messages, updating her Instagram and Facebook, while the couple next to them actually takes phone calls while at the restaurant. As the meal is served they leave the dinner holding hands until one of them receives another incoming text and he has to let go of her hand to pull his smartphone out of his pocket to respond to "one more message."

The man is scrolling through ESPN.com.

The woman is texting her friends and using Facebook.

Example #2

It's the business woman who never truly experiences restful sleep because she keeps her phone on and next to her bed 24 / 7 just in case her daughter from college calls. As the years go by the business woman begins to feel and look exhausted at all times because she has not created any digital boundaries.

1. Email - Your T-mobile bill for $113.82 has been processed.

2. Text - Hey Susan, call me in the morning before the meeting.

3. Missed Call - Hey Susan, we are calling to let you know that it has been 3 months since you last serviced your vehicle. Call us today if you would like to schedule a tune-up.

4. Email - Your Dropbox file has been shared.

5. Etc...

Example #3

It's the founder of a business who responds to text messages from friends, family and clients during his own staff meeting that he is supposed to be leading. As the team members watch their boss tune out mentally so do they. Soon the very purpose of the meeting comes into question.

Karl: Hey boss, what is your take on it? Should we cut the marketing department's budget or keep it as is?"

Boss: Could you repeat that?

Karl: Yeah, we just wanted to know if we should cut the marketing department's budget or keep it the same?

Boss: Guys, I'm sorry, I have to take this call.

Wife: Hey honey can you talk right now?

Boss: No, I'm in a meeting.

Example #4

It's the business owning family who continues to check their work email while on the beach in Florida while they are supposed to be vacationing with their kids. As they see the emails come in they are now aware of problems, yet they are powerless as they are on a beach with their kids who now feel neglected as they watch their parents become distracted yet again.

Doug: "Hey Susan can you talk?!"

Mom: "Yeah, but I'm at the beach so I can't really talk right now!?"

Doug: "Got it."

Mom: "Hey Doug, I'm at the beach so I don't have anything to write something down, but could you send me an email reminder of this conversation?!"

EXAMPLE #5

"A new study found that teenagers are increasingly depressed, feel hopeless and are more likely to consider suicide. Researchers found a sudden increase in teens' symptoms of depression, suicide risk factors and suicide rates in 2012."

Research continually shows how distracting cell phones are—so some schools want to ban them - https://www.cnbc.com/2019/01/18/research-shows-that-cell-phones-distract-students--so-france-banned-them-in-school--.html

In order for you to become triggered to win, you are going to have to have to MAKE ONE DRAMATIC CHANGE TODAY.

You are going to have to commit to using your smartphone as a helpful tool instead of allowing your smartphone to turn you into a tool.

Over the years as I've worked with small business owners to help them dramatically increase the size of their businesses and their overall levels of personal success, I've discovered that teaching people how to use their smartphone has been a critical first step in allowing them to begin gaining traction in this world of perpetual distraction.

In this world of endless distractions, you and I must become VERY intentional about being both mentally and physically present at the same time.

Help me to help you by answering the following questions by circling Yes or No.

Should you have your smartphone on while driving? (Yes or No)

Should you have your smartphone on while having sex? (Yes or No)

Should you be using your smartphone while attending a funeral? (Yes or No)

Should you have your smartphone on while talking to your love interest at a restaurant? (Yes or No)

Should players be checking their smartphone while actually sitting on the bench while playing in a National Basketball Association game? (Yes or No)

Should you be interacting with your smartphone while attending an office meeting? (Yes or No)

Should you be using your smartphone while sitting down to use the restroom?

Should you be utilizing your smartphone on while standing up to use the restroom? (Yes or No)

Should you have your smartphone on your while attending concerts? (Yes or No)

Should you be interacting with your smartphone while attending a church service? (Yes or No)

Should you have your smartphone on while watching a movie at a movie theatre? (Yes or No)

Should you have your smartphone phone on while attending a birthday party? (Yes or No)

Should you be using your smartphone to access adult content while serving in the United Kingdom's House of Commons or Parliament? (Yes or No)

https://www.huffingtonpost.co.uk/2013/09/03/
parliament-porn-websites_n_3859837.html?guccounter=1

Should you be using your smartphone while walking down the street? (Yes or No)

. . . .

Should you be using your smartphone at a family dinner? (Yes or No)

. . . .

Should you be using your smartphone while attending an educational class? (Yes or No)

. . . .

Should you be using your smartphone when someone is talking directly to you? (Yes or No)

. . . .

Should you be using your smartphone while working out? (Yes or No)

. . . .

Should you be using your smartphone while driving your car? (Yes or No)

. . . .

Should you use your smartphone while doing work at your job? (Yes or No)

. . . .

Should you be using your smartphone while watching your kids perform at their activity of choice? (gymnastics, swimming, cheerleading, basketball, ballet, football, baseball, hockey, etc.) (Yes or No)?

. . . .

Should you be using your smartphone while watching Jerry Seinfeld perform live (Yes or No)?

. . . .

Although I wish it weren't true, I consistently see men using their smartphone with one hand while holding their "device" while urinating, only to make things worse by leaving the restroom without washing their hands. Nearly EVERY time that I go out to eat, I see men and women out on dates with each other while spending their entire meal mentally out to lunch and lost somewhere in cyberspace. And although watching someone attempt to get on a treadmill while using their smartphone can be funny, I've also personally witnessed people nearly tumbling to a certain injury while attempting to text while getting onto the Stairmaster.

In this world of endless distractions, you and I must become VERY intentional about being both mentally and physically present at the same time. As an example, as I sat down to write this very chapter of this book, my smartphone is turned off and my mind is 100% focused on helping you to learn how to become the kind of momentum producing person that gets things done.

NOTABLE QUOTABLE

"It's hard to edit. It's hard to stay focused. And yet, we know we'll only do our best work if we stay focused. And so, you know, the hardest decisions we made are all the things not to work on, frankly."

TIM COOK
(The CEO of Apple)

The main reason that I am able to write this book and to be 100% focused on you is because I keep my phone off 90% of the time. Most of the time, my smartphone serves me best by being in "airplane mode."

In fact, I would highly recommend that you would take just a moment to decide the rare moments when you actually need to have your smartphone turned on:

Smartphone On Situations #1: _____

_____

Smartphone On Situations #2: _____

_____

Smartphone On Situations #3: _____

_____

Smartphone On Situations #4: _____

_____

Smartphone On Situations #5: _____

_____

Smartphone On Situations #6: _____

_____

Smartphone On Situations #7: _____

_____

Smartphone On Situations #8: _____

_____

Smartphone On Situations #9: _____

_____

In order to begin to achieve massive traction with your life and career you must begin to view distractions as being a time robber that is stealing your most important asset (time). Time is our most important asset because we cannot make more time, but we can make more money. It's time for you to identify the biggest wasters of your time and begin to say "no" to these time wasters as soon as possible. In fact, to help you, let me introduce you to the biggest time wasting activities that I have found to plague my clients before I help them learn how to become triggered to win.

- Watching TV
- Smartphone usage
- Updating and responding to social media
- Saying "Yes" to all invitations
- Endlessly checking your email
- Multi-tasking

Fact

"On average, American adults
are watching five hours and four
minutes of television per day."

https://www.nytimes.com/2016/07/01/business/
media/nielsen-survey-media-viewing.html

Throughout my career I've had the opportunity to interview countless millionaires and even a few billionaires and nearly every one of them does not watch TV or engage with social media on an ongoing basis. All research shows that most people are wasting their time watching TV and engaging on social media. Thus, it would seem logical to conclude that spending your day watching TV or engaging on social media is an epic waste of time and a profoundly sad waste of a life.

I have discovered that as a culture we are
all naturally "addicted to new" and that only
the masters, the greats and the icons of our
culture choose to bore down while the rest
of the world struggled with boredom.

Winners Throughout History Bore Down, The Rest Suffered from Boredom. The winners in our world are those who have chosen to become great at something by learning to say "no" to the endless distractions and opportunities swirling around them.

Nearly every day I receive an email, or a message of some kind from an entrepreneur with a "new idea" who is 100% passionately convinced that they have the skills needed to "change the world" and to make it a better place, if only I would be willing to invest my time and money into helping them turn their dreams into reality.

NOTABLE QUOTABLE

"People think focus means saying yes to the thing you've got to focus on. But that's not what it means at all. It means saying no to the hundred other good ideas that there are. You have to pick carefully. I'm actually as proud of the things we haven't done as the things I have done. Innovation is saying no to 1,000 things."

STEVE JOBS
(The co-founder of Apple, the founder of NeXT, and the former CEO of PIXAR)

However, here's the problem...I can always make more money, but I can't always make more time, and thus I have to choose whether I am going to help them to achieve their goals or whether I am going to maintain my focus on reaching the fulfillment of my own goals.

Initially, new ideas always sound exciting because we all love new things (new cars, new houses, new relationships, etc.).

However, over time having interviewed millionaires and billionaires on The *Thrivetime Show* while also building my own successful companies I have discovered that as a culture we are all naturally "addicted to new" and that only the masters, the greats and the icons of our culture choose to bore down while the rest of the world struggled with boredom.

Once you determine what you are going after, trade-up everything else. Bore down and don't stop until you achieve your goals!

NOTABLE QUOTABLE

"In the future, the great division will be between those who have trained themselves to handle these complexities and those who are overwhelmed by them -- those who can acquire skills and discipline their minds and those who are irrevocably distracted by all the media around them and can never focus enough to learn."

ROBERT GREENE, *MASTERY*

(The best-selling author of *Mastery, The 48 Laws of Power, the 50th Law*, etc.)

Fact

"American adults spend more than 11 hours per day watching, reading, listening to or simply interacting with media, according to a new study by market-research group Nielsen. That's up from nine hours, 32 minutes just four years ago."

- https://www.marketwatch.com/story/people-are-spending-most-of-their-waking-hours-staring-at-screens-2018-08-01

CHAPTER 6

DON'T ALLOW THE ALMOND-SIZED PART OF YOUR BRAIN TO CONTROL YOUR WHOLE LIFE

"USE YOUR SMARTPHONE AS A TOOL, BUT DON'T ALLOW IT TO USE YOU AS A TOOL."
- ME

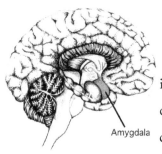

Amygdala

Because your smartphone is connected 24/7 to the world around you, your amygdala is now working overtime and you must decide here and now to stop allowing it to control your life. What is the amygdala? Your amygdala is one of the two almond-shaped parts of your brain that controls your emotional responses including aggression, anxiety, and fear. Your amygdala is the part of your brain that is put in charge of coping with sudden fear. Research shows that once your amygdala gets involved, it's very hard to make logical and unemotional based decisions.

> ### When you allow your smartphone to be on you at all times, you are allowing the world's worries, threats and problems to access you and impact how you see the world.

Ironically, in today's world if you are NOT VERY INTENTIONAL, smartphones and the endless connectivity to digital devices will leave you feeling disconnected while crowding out your optimism, proactivity, and thoughtfulness. Your smartphone is a relentless 24/7 distraction machine sent here on a mission to overwhelm you with information, updates, and push notifications. In fact, research is now showing (shockingly) that constant exposure to the world's most divisive political issues, negative news, and the endless waves of information is not good for you or your mental health. As an example, as I sat down to write this particular chapter of the book this morning before my kids wake up, I had the misfortune of discovering that the previous person to use my computer last visited CNN.com and had decided to leave the website page open before they left the office for today. Thus, before I could even begin writing this practical guide about how to trigger yourself to win, I first had to hear Rudy Guliani's take on why "There's nothing wrong with taking information from the Russians" and how "Weeks after (rapper) Nipsey Hussle's slaying still leaves many questions remaining".

NOTABLE QUOTABLE

"The mind is what the mind is fed."

DAVID J. SCHWARTZ

(The legendary and best-selling author of *The Magic of Thinking Big*)

Thus, today, before I decided to have a positive perspective about my day and started writing this book, negativity was pushed upon me by negative news. When you allow your smartphone to be on you at all times, you are allowing the world's worries, threats and problems to access you and impact how you see the world. Although modern medicine and science has dramatically improved the standard of living for the vast majority of the people on this planet, when I started my first business, DJConnection.com, in 1999, life was simpler. I believe it was easier to block out negativity back then.

Back in 1999, the distractions and temptations that we now all face were not at our fingertips 24/7. Now, before you begin to tell me why you can't disconnect from the internet and that new appendage that you call your smartphone consider these facts:

Smartphones cause perpetual digital distraction, disconnectedness from real life and dystopia.

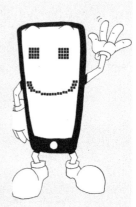

NOTABLE QUOTABLE

"Why I've never carried an iPhone. 'Our minds can be hijacked': the tech insiders who fear a smartphone dystopia. The Google, Apple and Facebook workers who helped make technology so addictive are disconnecting themselves from the internet."

- Our minds can be hijacked: *The tech insiders fear a smartphone dystopia.*" - Paul Lewis - *The Guardian*
https://www.theguardian.com/technology/2017/oct/05/smartphone-addiction-silicon-valley-dystopia

13 Terrifying Facts About Smartphone Use:

1. 9 people die per day (3,285 people die per year) as a result of distracted driving.
    https://www.cdc.gov/motorvehiclesafety/distracted_driving/index.html

2. 1,000 injury crashes per day are reported to involve a distracted driver.
    https://www.cdc.gov/motorvehiclesafety/distracted_driving/index.html

3. Parents who choose to attempt
    to parent their children while also
    using their smartphones are not
    fully present which overtime has
    been shown to create long-term
    emotional issues with children.

    Psychology Today. - https://www.businessinsider.
    com/12-ways-your-smartphone-is-making-
    your-life-worse-2018-6#7-some-people-base-
    their-self-worth-on-social-media-likes-7

4. The more you choose to use smart
    phones the more likely you are
    to experience depression.

    https://www.businessinsider.com/12-ways-your-
    smartphone-is-making-your-life-worse-2018-6#12-
    they-may-not-be-good-for-our-mental-health-12

5. Smartphone usage puts you at a
    higher risk for cyberbullying.

    https://www.cbc.ca/life/wellness/your-kids-
    smartphones-may-be-putting-them-at-a-
    higher-risk-for-cyberbullying-1.4348254

6. Research conclusively shows that
    your memory, mental capacity
    and overall ability to process data
    improves dramatically when a
    smartphone is out of your sight.

    https://www.psychologytoday.com/us/
    blog/startup-your-life/201801/why-your-
    smartphone-is-destroying-your-life

7. Research shows that when you have
    a smartphone that is visible in a social
    setting it dramatically decreases the
    quality of the interaction, which creates
    more bogus and superficial social
    interactions.

    https://www.psychologytoday.com/us/
    blog/startup-your-life/201801/why-your-
    smartphone-is-destroying-your-life

8. Studies now prove that you will sleep less well when you have a smartphone that is left next to you while you are sleeping.

https://www.businessinsider.com/12-ways-your-smartphone-is-making-your-life-worse-2018-6#1-smartphones-contribute-to-sleep-issues-1

9. It is now a proven fact that the average person interacts with their smartphone at least 85 times per day, which makes it impossible for most people to now hold a deep thought or to engage in an authentic conversation.

https://www.psychologytoday.com/us/blog/startup-your-life/201801/why-your-smartphone-is-destroying-your-life

10. Since the proliferation of the smartphone, the Center for Disease Control shows that life expectancy is down as more Americans die younger due to suicide and drug overdose

https://www.cbsnews.com/news/cdc-us-life-expectancy-declining-due-largely-to-drug-overdose-and-suicides

11. People who use a smartphone non-stop have been shown to have more chronic hand, neck, and back issues. In fact anxiety, depression, disrupted sleep, diminished attention span, antisocial behavior, decreased empathy are all attributed to today's average smartphone use."

https://www.psychologytoday.com/us/blog/startup-your-life/201801/why-your-smartphone-is-destroying-your-life

12. Next time you go out to a restaurant and look at the lack of interaction and eye contact being had by couples who are out to eat. It turns out that the person you are on a date with will not like going out with you if you spend more time on your smartphone than you spend paying attention to them.

   https://www.businessinsider.com/12-ways-your-smartphone-is-making-your-life-worse-2018-6#2-they-can-ruin-romantic-relationships-2

13. Since social media was created many people now cannot help from comparing themselves to the people that they see earning likes and shares on social media.

   https://www.businessinsider.com/12-ways-your-smartphone-is-making-your-life-worse-2018-6#7-some-people-base-their-self-worth-on-social-media-likes-7

Smartphones allow people to experience a near insatiable fear of missing out (FOMO) regardless of how great what you are actually doing may be.

Smartphones dramatically decrease your ability to retain what you are reading if you choose to do your reading while on a smartphone.

Kids who spend more time on screens tend to be significantly less happy than kids who engage in non-screen related activities like playing sports, engaging with tangible printed materials, or spending time socializing with real people in real life.

http://time.com/5437607/smartphones-teens-mental-health/

The smartphone now allows you to have real-time access to constant threats, political disagreements, divisive religious arguments, disgruntled employees and former friends that are all just one ping away from stealing our joy. So, the time to disconnect from the negative news headlines that are crowding out your positivity and optimism is now. But how do you do this? I would like to offer 6 specific steps for you to take today to help you trade-up your smartphone for something better, and free you from the digital distractions that are wasting your time.

Fact
The world is actually getting better. According to research published by The Atlantic, the life expectancy of someone born during 1800 was 39.4 years and now someone born during the 1980s is well over 70 years of age.
https://www.theatlantic.com/magazine/
archive/2013/11/die-another-day/309541/

STEP 1 - Keep Your Phone Off 90% of the Time

If you want to develop deep relationships, have deep thoughts, and to develop deep pockets, keep your phone off 90% of the day or store your phone somewhere deep and far away when you are not using it. When you are on a date with a potential love-interest, brush and floss your teeth thoroughly, show up 15 minutes early to pick them up, and be 100% mentally present on that date. Don't check your emails, text messages, and social media updates while waiting for the food or you will find yourself in the perpetual dog house. Everybody can see you texting underneath the table, so don't even pretend that this is a secret "super move" that you can discreetly use without humanity noticing. My go to quote to people I see on their smartphone while at dinner or hanging out is "if you're going to be here... BE HERE."

NOTABLE QUOTABLE

"I've never carried an iPhone."

PAUL GRAHAM

(The founder of Viaweb which was later sold to Yahoo! For $49.6 million and was renamed Yahoo! Store. Paul is also the man who founded the entrepreneurial incubator known as Y Cominator which has now invested in over 1,300 startups including Dropbox.com, Airbnb, Reddit and Stripe.)

IM PAUL GRAHAM
& I DON'T CARRY
A SMART PHONE

Step 2 - Create Both Digital and Personal Boundaries for Your Life

Just before I sold DJConnection.com, we were literally providing entertainment services for thousands of brides and grooms per year, and I had failed to create digital boundaries for both myself and my family so our clients and the soon-to-be married couples, who were super-excited to get married, called me personally at all times. Through repeated interactions, I had trained our customers to believe that I was always available to meet their needs.

I can remember enduring multiple Sundays where brides-to-be would just show up at our doorstep at 8900 South Lynn Lane, Broken Arrow, OK without an appointment just to "check-in" or to "confirm that we had them on the books." Although I was frustrated that my wife and I were never allowed to enjoy downtime as a couple because our customers would endlessly interrupt us, it was really me that I was frustrated the most with.

Because I had refused to create digital boundaries for myself, I had created a type of financially lucrative dystopia that I would not wish on anyone. Every hour of every day I was available for anyone that needed to reach me other than my wife, my kids, and the people that mattered most.

ACTION ITEM: Define your boundaries. When do you want your friends, family and clients to be able to reach you? When do you want to be unreachable? _____

Step 3 - Stop Feeling the Need to

Call or "Ping" People Back Simply Because They Called You.

Although the good folks at Target, Bed Bath and Beyond and Victoria Secret are tremendous humans, I don't feel the need to call them back to let them know that I am rejecting their most recent mass-mailer offer and that I will not be coming in their store with my wife to buy 3 panties to get the 4th one free. Also you and I shouldn't feel the need to call everyone back who calls us. Additionally, don't try to respond to all social media updates, messages, or comments that you receive either. In this world of 24/7 connection to everybody, by default you will lose connection with what matters most if you are not intentional about not responding to the digital interactions that do not matter.

NOTABLE QUOTABLE

"Tryin' to disconnect, thinking maybe you could show me If there's so many people here, then why am I so lonely?"

RYAN TEDDER

(Grammy award-winning artist and the frontman for OneRepublic)

Step 4 - Stop Responding to Things That Don't Matter

During the short amount of time that you and I get to enjoy on the planet Earth, we all have goals, and items that we want to experience, and unless you are a real sick freak, I doubt that the following items are currently listed as "big goals" or "bucket list items" for your life:

Spend my life responding to the random emails sent by people that I don't know or have a relationship with.

Spend my life responding to Facebook friend invites from people who barely know people that I barely know.

Interact with people on Youtube who strongly dislike the videos that I just produced.

Argue with someone that I don't know via Instagram or Twitter.

Get into heated political or religious debates

online with people I have never met

. . . .

Dear Self,

As of October 13th 2019, I am not going to settle for mediocrity anymore. In fact I here and now vow that I will accomplish the following goals this week:

I will spend 2 hours per day responding to random emails sent by people that I don't know or have a relationship with.

I will spend at least 5 hours this week responding to Facebook friend invites from people who barely know people that I barely know and commenting on things.

I will leave harsh comments about the Youtube videos created by others and I will block out time to respond to the negative comments left by others.

I will argue with someone that I don't know via Instagram or Twitter.

I will block out at least 2 hours this week to get into heated political or religious debates online with people I have never met.

NAVEN JOHNSON

Step 5 - Schedule Time for What Matters Most

In order to increase our overall levels of happiness and to become successful on the planet Earth you must choose to block out time in your schedule for the events that matter most to you including:

When are you scheduling time for the practicing of your faith?

. . . .

When are you scheduling time for your family?

. . . .

When are you scheduling time for the earning of your financial success?

. . . .

When you are you scheduling time for the maintenance of your physical fitness?

. . . .

When are you scheduling time to invest in the friendships that matter most to you?

. . . .

When are you scheduling time to engage in the activities that you believe to be fun?

. . . .

NOTABLE QUOTABLE

"People think focus means saying yes to the thing you've got to focus on. But that's not what it means at all. It means saying no to the hundred other good ideas that there are. You have to pick carefully. I'm actually as proud of the things we haven't done as the things I have done. Innovation is saying no to 1,000 things."

STEVE JOBS

(The co-founder of Apple, the founder of NeXT, and the former CEO of PIXAR)

Step 6 - Don't Allow Yourself to Become a Tool of Social Media Tools

Social media is not true life, it is a place where people go to post their kernels of corn out of the vomit of life. Without being intentional about saying "no" to the distractions that are standing in the way of you having the time and mental capacity needed to take actions that will help you to gain traction with your life and career, you will become just another asset and powerful selling statistic. In the world of social media, you are the product on your social media that social media companies use to sell companies the value of advertising online. You must commit RIGHT HERE AND NOW that social media is important to use because

_____ and _____.

If after thinking about it you now have determined that social media is a waste of time for you and your family then I would encourage you to cancel and shut down your accounts today. You and I must remember that the distractions standing in the way of the achievement of our goals are merely unnecessary wastes of time. I empower, encourage, and highly endorse that you should disengage from social media if it is not helping you to get closer to the achievement of your goals.

Fact

"Teens are spending more than one-third of their days using media such as online video or music — nearly nine hours on average, according to a new study from the family technology education non-profit group, Common Sense Media. For tweens, those between the ages of 8 and 12, the average is nearly six hours per day."

-Teens spend nearly nine hours every day consuming media - https://www.washingtonpost. com/news/the-switch/wp/2015/11/03/teens-spend-nearly-nine-hours-every-day-consuming-media/?noredirect=on&utm_term=.bef05bf6dcc6

SKYLER: "DUDE, COULD YOU PASS ME THE REMOTE?"

MADISON: "OK."

SKYLER: "MADISON, ARE YOU HUNGRY?"

MADISON: "YEP."

SKYLER: "LET'S ORDER SOME DOOR DASH."

CHAPTER 1

DON'T LET THE TROLLS BE IN CONTROL

Having grown up with limited financial resources and having started my first business DJConnection.com, out of my Oral Roberts University college dorm room, I can tell you with 100% confidence that "success is a choice that requires trade-ups." This is why in a world where Forbes reports that 9 out of 10 startups fail, I have been able to build several million dollar businesses without having a college degree, a rich family or good looks (or even average looks). Working towards this success has required me to completely tune out trolls that try to distract me.

FUN FACT:

"90% of startups fail."
- https://www.forbes.com/sites/neilpatel/2015/01/16/90-
of-startups-will-fail-heres-what-you-need-
to-know-about-the-10/#4d9cc7996679

Although I'm not Lebron James, or Oprah Winfrey, I have been happily married to the same woman for 19 years, I'm a father of 5 kids, the founder / co-founder of multiple successful companies (EITRLounge.com, MakeYourLifeEpic.com, DJConnection.com, etc.), the author of _____ books, and the co-host of the daily "Business School without the BS: podcast called The *Thrivetime Show*. Despite coming from a background of limited financial means and without the investment of a rich family member, I've found a way to gain significant traction with both my personal life and career and I know that you can too. This never would have happened if I cared about the trolls of this world.

NOTABLE QUOTABLE

"Whatever is begun in anger, ends in shame."

BENJAMIN FRANKLIN

(The famous American polymath, founding father, postmaster, scientist, inventor, writer, and diplomat who was able to get alot of things done during his lifetime)

In our current culture, everybody has now been given a voice and a place to share their world views with the entire world via social media platforms, blogs, vlogs, the comments section found below Youtube videos, online newspaper articles, etc. However, by default, you don't have to take the time out of your day to allow the "trolls to be in control of your emotions and your soul." As you begin to be more and more intentional about how and where you spend your time, you must understand that increasingly, the trolls will be in control of your life if you let them.

As an example, years ago one of the members of our team was convicted of selling drugs and was sent to Federal prison for doing so. It was my decision to sever all ties with him as a result of his decision to repeatedly sell drugs and to become a deadbeat father. And, although I believe that for a multitude of reasons my decision to cut this long-time employee out of my life was justified, many people in my life at the time simply could not understand:

Why would you not return his calls?

Why did you block him from your phone?

Why did you refuse to meet him when
he was released from prison?

Why did you not want to speak to him?

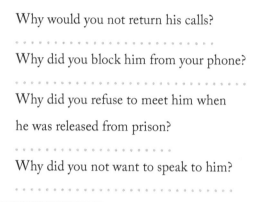

To improve the quality of your life by 2% I have invested the time needed to provide you with a quick list of the 10 common denominators related to internet trolls

Throughout my career as a business owner I have often taken the stance that anybody who chooses to have an affair with another man's wife is not the kind of person that I want working within my organization. Yet, many trollish and unsuccessful people can't understand this and they will ask me questions like:

Why would you not return their calls?

Why did you block him from your phone?

Why did you refuse to meet him

to discuss what happened?

Why did you not want to speak to them?

NOTABLE QUOTABLE

"Never react emotionally to criticism. Analyze yourself to determine whether it is justified. If it is, correct yourself. Otherwise, go on about your business."

NORMAN VINCENT PEALE

(The best-selling author of *The Power of Positive Thinking* and *An American Minister*)

Soon, the trolls realized that they were not making progress in convincing me to invest my time meeting with felons and adulterers and so they did what trolls do. Trolls love to storm Reddit, Glassdoor and any other place on the internet that allow anonymous, highly-opinionated and low-character trolls to be in control and to have a platform to throw rocks at those of us who have chosen to be diligent and consistent over the long-haul.

So, how do you know if you are dealing with internet trolls and not sincere people who actually want to improve the world around them by baring their soul while using an anonymous screen name? To improve the quality of your life by 2% I have invested the time needed to provide you with a quick list of the 10 common denominators related to internet trolls so that you can immediately move on once you encounter someone who is attacking you or those that you care about.

**A man in his 30s sitting on the couch living in his mom's basement, yelling "Mom! When are you going to bring down those Hot Pockets? I'm hungry!"

**This man is also simultaneously writing a bad review about a restaurant while he's yelling for his mom.

** Thur service wudn't good. They weren't accurrut with my order.

Ridiculous screen names - Internet trolls tend to use screen names that reflect their trollishness - Sarah6969 is probably not the most credible profile on the internet.

They are legal experts without the degrees or certifications needed to prove that they know what they are talking about. Trolls love to paraphrase various portions of documents used by our Founding Fathers to create this great country including: random excerpts from the U.S. Constitution, the Federalist Papers, the Bible, etc. to make points that no one with a sound mind could argue with.

> ## Internet trolls tend to quote problem-plagued celebrities, socialists, musicians, and communists while arguing a point that anyone who has a basic understanding of how capitalism works would disagree with.

Internet trolls tend to develop strong opinions that they believe to be facts based upon poorly written blogs and poorly created Youtube videos created by other internet trolls.

Trolls believe they are misunderstood and underpaid gurus that society has yet to recognize. Trolls are typically unemployed and underappreciated (in their mind) which is why they typically have the time needed to write the four page spelling-error filled complaints about you and your business.

Third-party knowledge of everything - Internet trolls also know someone who knows someone who knows something about the real situation that they are discussing. Internet trolls rarely disclose their sources, because they don't have any real vetted sources to cite for the vast majority of their strong opinions and deeply flawed belief systems.

Poorly posted internet profiles - The internet's troll community doesn't seem to ever be able to find the time needed to fully fill out their internet or social media profiles. All of their accounts seem to be half-complete and the portions of their profiles that are complete seem to be half-baked which makes sense because they are usually half-baked (high) when creating their profiles.

Keyword warriors who are real life cowards - Internet trolls tend to be the cowards in real life, yet on the internet they are "keyboard warriors" who aggressively attack anyone on the planet who is doing something. Internet trolls love to bully businesses, people and organizations while hiding behind their computers and their anonymous user accounts.

They can't do basic math - Internet trolls are not good at basic math and they love to quote statistics from obscure websites created by other trolls. Trolls specialize in speaking only in the hyperbole that they create for the sole purpose of aggravating people who are intentional about their lives and who have chosen to consistently hold a job for the past decade or more.

Unapologetically bad grammar and spelling whenever possible - Internet trolls are too busy attacking you, people that are actually doing something and organizations that are doing something to invest the time needed to capitalize things correctly, to use commas and to spell anything correctly.

> **In order to minimize your interaction with internet trolls I would suggest that you would implement the following 4 action steps:**

1. Turn off your push notifications so that you are not immediately updated every time someone complains about you or writes a bad comment about your organization. If you don't do this you will find yourself living in a perpetual dystopia as your business grows.

2. Turn off the "commenting" option when possible on the various social media and website posting platforms to minimize the probability that the trolls will fill up the comment section of your content with the hate and negativity that they specialize in creating.

3. Always take the high-road when responding. I realize that this is easier said than done, but when you attack a troll, most consumers struggle to determine who is the real troll involved in the situation and they will tend to side with the person whose comments appear to be the most measured, calm and reasonable.

Cut the trolls out of your life for good. I have found that burning bridges is a great way to create the distance needed to design the life I love.

Thus, take a moment today and ceremoniously de-friend the continual sources of negativity in your life and on your social media. When doing this, remember that the friends of your enemies are you enemies and that you must remove the people and sources of negativity from your daily life if you want to maximize your happiness.

Stop wasting time with trolls! Make the trade-ups needed to get rid of them and free yourself to have total control of your focus and actions.

CHAPTER 8

SMARTPHONE FASTING - THE POWER OF WEEKLY DIGITAL DETOXING

NOTABLE QUOTABLE -

"Turn off your email; turn off your phone; disconnect from the Internet; figure out a way to set limits so you can concentrate when you need to, and disengage when you need to. Technology is a good servant but a bad master."

GRETCHEN RUBIN

(The *New York Times* best-selling author *The Happiness Project: Or Why I Spent a Year Trying to Sing in the Morning,* **Clean** My Closets, Fight Right, Read Aristotle, and Generally Have More Fun and 8 other incredible books)

BILLY: KARL, DON'T TURN OFF YOUR PHONE YOU MAY DIE!

KARL: BILLY, IT'S WORTH TO ME, I JUST HAVE TO TAKE THAT CHANCE.

BILLY: NO KARL! I LOVE YOU! STOP!!!!!! DON'T DO IT!!!!

When I am reachable 100% of the time, I will learn about an employee who is upset about something, a customer who doesn't like something, a review that is not positive or somebody that urgently needs to talk because "their life depends upon it" (the ultimate pressure statement).

No one can argue that our minds are now being bombarded with interruptions at a rate that is not healthy. When you and I look down at the text message we just received while driving, we are 23 times more likely to crash in an auto accident. Research conducted by the Florida State University is now showing a strong correlation between suicidal thinking and cellphone use and researchers are now showing that checking Facebook has been proven to make adults depressed, which is why I would recommend that you would engage in a digital detox once per week. What? Am I actually encouraging you to turn off your smartphone that is making us all impossibly distracted and depressed for at least 24 hours per week? Yes.

Fact

"Sending a text takes 5 seconds of your attention. You may be as much as 23 times more likely to crash and the risk is the same whether you type or "voice text."
https://www.nytimes.com/2009/07/28/technology/28texting.html

Fact

"Checking Facebook has been proven to make young adults depressed. Researchers who've studied college students' emotional well-being find a direct link: the more often people check Facebook, the more miserable they are. But the incessant, misery-inducing phone checking doesn't just stop there. Games like Fortnite or apps like Twitter can be addictive, in the sense that they will leave your brain craving another hit."
- https://www.businessinsider.com/what-your-smartphone-is-doing-to-your-brain-and-it-isnt-good-2018-3

Fact

"A study recently released by Florida State University showed a strong correlation between suicidal thinking and cellphone use, with those who used electronic devices for more than five hours per day showing close to a 50 percent incidence of at least one suicidal behavior."

- https://www.foxnews.com/opinion/dr-marc-siegel-smartphones-really-are-dangerous-for-our-kids-they-put-them-at-risk-for-suicide-and-more

In fact, as I have been writing this very section of the book you are reading now my phone has been turned off since Friday and it's now Sunday. What!? How is it possible!? Aren't I worried what could possibly happen if somebody wasn't able to reach me? No. In fact, I'm more worried about what will happen 100% of the time when people can reach me. When I am reachable 100% of the time, I will learn about an employee who is upset about something, a customer who doesn't like something, a review that is not positive or somebody that urgently needs to talk because "their life depends upon it" (the ultimate pressure statement).

When your phone is turned off you will find that your ability to focus, to communicate and to truly engage with people will dramatically improve and you will find that your overall level of anxiety will go down.

I sincerely know that I would not be able to write this book or any of the other books that I have written if my phone was kept on my desk face up as I was writing. It would simply be impossible for me to get into any type of writing flow, to organize my thoughts or to get anything done if the constant interruptions or fear of interruptions were only just a text, call, email, social media update or push notification away. I trade-up addiction to my smartphone for the freedom to create books like this and work towards my F6 goals without distractions. You can too!

Fact

"Most modern people spend a full quarter of their waking hours on their mobile device. According to one of the studies, about half the time (1 hour, 56 minutes) is spent on the top five social media platforms: Facebook, Instagram, Twitter, Snapchat, and YouTube."

- https://www.nielsen.com/us/en/insights/news/2018/time-flies-us-adults-now-spend-nearly-half-a-day-interacting-with-media.print.html

Although your "Nomophobia" may be real (your fear of No Mobile Phone Phobia), I promise that you will feel refreshed when you escape the soul-sucking cycle of receiving and responding to the 80 interruptions per day that we now all get according to research published by Psychology Today.

When your phone is turned off you will find that your ability to focus, to communicate and to truly engage with people will dramatically improve and you will find that your overall level of anxiety will go down.

Fact

"But our bodies have a different view: These constant alerts jolt our stress hormones into action, igniting our fight or flight response; our heartbeats quicken, our breathing tightens, our sweat glands burst open, and our muscles contract. That response is intended to help us outrun danger, not answer a call or text from a colleague."

- https://www.businessinsider.com/ what-your-smartphone-is-doing-to-your-brain-and-it-isnt-good-2018-3

CHAPTER 9

F.O.C.U.S. ON TRACTION PRODUCING ACTIVITIES

NOTABLE QUOTABLE

"Vision without execution is hallucination."

THOMAS EDISON

(The man who is credited with having invented the first practical modern lightbulb, recorded audio, and recorded video all while also starting General Electric)

Step 1 - Take a shower and get ready for work

Step 2 - Drive to work

Step 3 - Spend 11 hours interacting with digital media

Step 4 - Turn off FoxNews or CNN and get outraged about something that I can't control

Step 5 - God to bed

Each day, when I wake up, I write down the action steps that I can take that will get me and my family closer to the achievement of the goals we have for our faith, family, finances, fitness, friendship and fun. I invite you to do the same. It's amazing how much progress you can truly make in just one year's time if you truly take the time out of your schedule every day to plan out each and every day.

As an example, as it relates to our family, I have blocked out family time into our schedule to occur every Sunday night (preferably at 6 PM). I block out time for this family time, because if not by default our family would drift apart and we would go months and months without truly seeing and connecting with each other. In the area of friendships, I am very intentional about scheduling time to invest in developing the relationships that matter to me and I am also just as intentional about avoiding the physical presence and the communications of many people as well. Writing a book like this just doesn't happen. You and I must learn to block out the necessary time needed to create traction and success in our lives, to write your books, to create your business plans, to train your staff and to turn your dreams into reality. You must F.O.C.U.S.!

Fact
"According to the first-quarter 2018 Nielsen Total Audience Report, nearly half an adults' day is dedicated to consuming this content. In fact, American adults spend over 11 hours per day listening to, watching, reading or generally interacting with media."

- https://www.nielsen.com/us/en/insights/news/2018/time-flies-us-adults-now-spend-nearly-half-a-day-interacting-with-media.print.html

You and I know this to be true, but yet I think that you might need a WAKE-UP CALL, "There is no someday." You could spend the rest of your life looking for someday on the standard calendar, but you just won't ever find it. In your calendar and in mine, we will only find: Monday, Tuesday, Wednesday, Thursday, Friday, Saturday and Sunday.

There is no someday and the time to act is now. Trade-up distractions in order to F.O.C.U.S.!

NOTABLE QUOTABLE

"The way to get started is to quit talking and begin doing."

WALT DISNEY

(The co-founder of the Walt Disney empire)

CHAPTER 10

START NOW, SOME DAY IS NOT IN YOUR CALENDAR

Having personally worked with hundreds and hundreds of clients to help them achieve their ultimate success, I have found that when you do hard things, life gets easier. One of the hardest things for people to do is to say "no" to people and to the endless sources of distraction all around us. We don't want to say "no" because we don't want to hurt someone's feelings, or because we have been a member of this club or of that club for years or because we don't want to offend the person asking for our time. However, I am telling you that if you are like most people you are already very busy.

"If I turn my push notifications off, will my brain explode?!"

In order to get ahead in this game of life you are going to have to take a long and hard look at your life and to ask yourself what things you need to start saying "no" to so that you can trade-up to the best.

You can start to trade-up to the best things today. Start trading-up today and finally find traction in this world of endless distraction!

When I first really began focusing on becoming intentional about where and who I spent my time with, everything began to change. When I quit hanging out with the "intramural athletes" at Oral Roberts University I was able to get nearly 10 hours of my weeks back each week. When I worked at Applebee's, Target and DirecTV, I found that choosing to use my lunch breaks as my opportunity to call my company's leads changed my life, because it was the only down-time I had during the week to actually call my leads there for a while. When I decided to begin getting up at 3 AM everyday, it required me to trade-up staying up late with my roommate.

When I began to reinvest heavily into the $2,500 per month Yellow Page advertisements that I launched in order to grow DJConnection.com, Vanessa and I had to trade-up air-conditioning, and hanging out with certain drifting and non-purposeful friendships. When I chose to write this book, I had to choose to trade-up the constant smartphone calls, emails, social media updates and push notifications that are undoubtedly piling up on my phone as I write this practical book designed to help you. You can start to trade-up to the best things today. Start trading-up today and finally find traction in this world of endless distraction!

NOTABLE QUOTABLE

"People think focus means saying yes to the thing you've got to focus on. But that's not what it means at all. It means saying no to the hundred other good ideas that there are. You have to pick carefully. I'm actually as proud of the things we haven't done as the things I have done. Innovation is saying no to 1,000 things."

STEVE JOBS

(The co-founder of Apple, the former CEO of PIXAR and the founder of NeXT)

Want to Take Your Life and Business to Next Level?

Listen to our chart-topping business school without the BS podcast today and everyday at www.ThrivetimeShow.com. Over the years we have interviewed millionaires, billionaires and everyday success stories including (but not limited to):

8x *New York Times* Best-Selling Author and
Leadership Expert, John Maxwell

Celebrity Chef, Entrepreneur, and *New York Times*
Best-Selling Author, Wolfgang Puck

Legendary Former Key Apple Employee Turned Venture
Capitalist, Best Selling Author, Guy Kawasaki

New York Times Best-Selling Co-Author of Rich
Dad Poor Dad, Sharon Lechter

Senior pastor of the largest church in America with over 100,000
weekly attendees (Lifechurch.tv), Craig Groeschel

One of America's most trusted financial experts and
has written nine consecutive *New York Times* bestsellers
with 7 million+ books in print, David Bach

NBA Hall of Famer, David Robinson (2-time NBA
Champion, 2-time Gold Medal Winner)

Senior Editor for *Forbes* and 3x Best-Selling Author, Zack O'Malley Greenburg

Most Downloaded Business Podcaster of All-Time (EOFire.com), John Lee Dumas

New York Times Best-Selling Author of *Purple Cow*, and former Yahoo! Vice President of Marketing, Seth Godin

Co-Founder of the 700+ Employee Advertising Company (AdRoll), Adam Berke

Emmy Award-winning Producer of the *Today Show* and *New York Times* Best-Selling Author of *Sh*tty Moms,* Mary Ann Zoellner

New York Times Best-Selling Author of *Contagious: Why Things Catch On* and Wharton Business Professor, Jonah Berger

New York Times Best-Selling Author of *Made to Stick* and Duke University Professor, Dan Heath

WANT TO KNOW EVEN MORE?
CHECK OUT ALL OF CLAY'S BOOKS

START HERE

The World's Best Business Growth & Consulting Book: Business Growth Strategies from the World's Best Business Coach.

DON'T LET YOUR EMPLOYEES HOLD YOU HOSTAGE

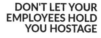

This candid book shares how to avoid being held hostage by employees.

F6 JOURNAL

Meta Thrive Time Journal.

THE ENTREPRENEUR'S DRAGON ENERGY

The Mindset Kanye, Trump and You Need to Succeed.

BOOM

The 13 Proven Steps to Business Success.

MAKE YOUR LIFE EPIC

Clay shares his journey and struggle from the dorm room to the board room during his raw and action-packed story of how he built DJConnection.com.

JACKASSARY

Jackassery will serve as a beacon of light for other entrepreneurs that are looking to avoid troublesome employees and difficult situations. This is real. This is raw. This is unfiltered entrepreneurship.

THE ART OF GETTING THINGS DONE

Clay Clark breaks down the proven, time-tested and time freedom creating super moves that you can use to create both the time freedom and financial freedom that most people only dream about.

THRIVE

How to Take Control of Your Destiny and Move Beyond Surviving... Now!

WILL NOT WORK FOR FOOD

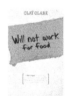

9 Big Ideas for Effectively Managing Your Business in an Increasingly Dumb, Distracted & Dishonest America

PODCAST DOMINATION

This book will show you how to prepare, record, launch, and begin generating income from your podcast, all from your home studio!

SEARCH ENGINE DOMINATION

Learn the Proven System We've Used to Earn Millions.

WHEEL OF WEALTH

An Entrepreneur's Action Guide.